New Poetries III

MICHAEL SCHMIDT is Director of the Writing School at Manchester Metropolitan University, author of *Lives of the Poets* (Weidenfeld, 1998) and editor of *The Harvill Book of Twentieth-Century Poetry in English* (1999) and of *The Story of Poetry: From Caedmon to Caxton* (2001). He also edited *New Poetries* and *New Poetries II*.

Also available from Carcanet

New Poetries
New Poetries II

New Poetries III

Edited by Michael Schmidt

CARCANET

First published in Great Britain in 2002 by
Carcanet Press Limited
4th Floor, Conavon Court
12–16 Blackfriars Street
Manchester M3 5BQ

A CIP catalogue record for this book
is available from the British Library
ISBN trade paperback edition 1 85754 592 3

The publisher acknowledges financial assistance
from the Arts Council of England

Set in Monotype Bembo by XL Publishing Services, Tiverton
Printed and bound in England by SRP Ltd, Exeter

CONTENTS

INTRODUCTION

A French critic, François Lyotard perhaps, suggests that one radical way of disrupting a category, destabilising its inherent ideology and either changing it or rendering it inert, is to stuff it to bursting point. Take a literary canon, for example. It is patriarchal, so the work of women must be added, an act both of just restitution and, in most cases, of aesthetic enrichment. Then there is the issue of accommodating ethnicities, and the forms peculiar to them. There is, also, the question of gender and gender-preference. With each addition the aesthetic imperatives are stretched further and further, becoming frail until, eventually, the canon is so vast as to be meaningless. The earlier criteria of inclusion look ridiculous because they excluded so much, and the works those criteria privileged now look, like the white protestant male, exposed, goose-fleshed and not a little chagrined.

The strategy is directly political in effect: it does not so much redefine as undefine. Where there is no definition, there is no hierarchy, no best or worst. The general public quite like this because it flatters them: the dreaded word 'elitism' is discredited, and what is difficult or obscure need not detain us. The approach is enriching to a degree, working against prejudice. In another sense, crudely implemented, it can be impoverishing. Indeed, it can, as definition is erased, take on the features of the political and ethical ideologies to which initially it responded antithetically.

The problem is most apparent when we examine the rhetoric of liberal multiculturalism. Multiculturalism itself has been immensely enriching to our societies and cultures. It is, however, as a token term with an increasingly authoritarian rhetoric attached to it, becoming illiberal not only as it relates to the older traditions it seeks to open out, but also those cultures it strives to accommodate. A recent instance of this was the addition of the performance poetry of Linton Kwesi Johnson to the Penguin Classics list, and the ways in which the media dealt with the issue.

Linton Kwesi Johnson is a leading performance poet. He has a band, his poetry is specific to his voice, his choreography, his manner of performing. Its inclusion in the Penguin Classics list is inappropriate. A respect for Penguin Classics and the definition of the classic they embody, as well as a respect for the medium in which Johnson works, make it necessary to say that the appropriation of performance texts, unstable as they necessarily are given that they change with each performance context, and that they depend on a specific *performing* voice, is inappropriate. John Clare was dressed up, taken to London and paraded as an Augustan bumpkin.

We recoil from the condescension and patronage to which he was subjected and to the cruel withdrawal of that patronage when the poet evinced real needs. The inclusion of D.H. Lawrence's poems in Edward Marsh's *Georgian Anthologies* was a piece of editorial misjudgement or mischievous appropriation.

The word 'classic' has specific meanings and implications, none of them to do primarily with popularity or range of appeal. Penguin Classics come close to the present in the work they include but in general acknowledge that a classic has already endured; a text can only become classic when it is stable, that is, when the author is no longer there to alter it. It would have strained the classic category had Robert Lowell, reviser *par excellence*, or David Jones, or W.H. Auden been admitted in their lifetimes. A living classic is put to death as soon as classic status is conferred. The text is set in stone. Several generations of schoolchildren read selections of Ted Hughes and Thom Gunn and never had an inkling that *Crow* or *Moly* had occurred. Both poets stayed in the happy time-warp of their late twenties for decades, and they weren't even called 'Classics', though 'set text' is the next category down.

Kwesi Johnson was added to the Penguin Classics list because the editors rightly believe that a powerful Caribbean contribution to British culture since the 1950s is in the area of performance, the rapid-fire, political and highly rhythmic rap. It is important to acknowledge that contribution, and Linton Kwesi Johnson is a real performer.

But is his work compelling on the page? His admirers insist that it is, that it has prosodic coherence and semantic depth. Yet anyone who has not heard Johnson perform in his own voice will find it hard to read the poems from the page, and to scan those which have more or less regular stress patterns. The technique is in the voice which compensates for a missing beat, an inefficient inversion, a short or over-length line, an awkward rhyme. The in-print difficulty is common to much performance poetry: it is compelling on stage, CD or video, but the silent libretto is inert. As for semantic depth: no. There are puns, there's word-play, cliches and reanimated cliches, postures are forcefully struck. But the language does not develop ideas (the ideas precede composition and are not always original); it is language composed to affect an audience.

Having acknowledged the impact of performance poetry, the next step, the method of acknowledgement and inclusion, works against respect and genuine multiculturalism. A largely white, liberal establishment, wishing to celebrate a challenging phenomenon, 'applies familiar templates to the unfamiliar', transposes it into a familiar medium that degrades and denatures it. A Penguin Classic CD (with a booklet providing texts) or video would have been appropriate media. But stripped of the backing group, the audience, with the voice silenced and folded into the prematurely grey pages of a Penguin Classic, the work has been appropriated. It is sold: this is clearly not what the work is or aspires to be.

Multiculturalism fails when it falsifies genres. This form of institution-alised misunderstanding proceeds from a mixture of political and cultural imperatives. Some editors have the courage to concede as much, though seldom in public. What is urgently needed, if multiculturalism is not to become a form of bland relativism, a meeting-place where positive differ-ence is airbrushed out and creative debate and conflict are stilled, is an ability to understand formal and generic differences, and the inventiveness to find the right medium for each 'manifestation'. The acknowledgement of what is new and unexpected in our culture is not served by false taxonomies. They are an aspect of that 'repressive tolerance' which those of us who were radical in the 1960s strongly opposed. Cultural conser-vatism strives to re-establish security through denial; false taxonomies are as pernicious, denying us the instruction, pleasure and extension that come from acknowledged and understood differences in mediums and genres.

★ ★ ★

The blurring and erasure of definitions affects the emergence of new voices. How does a new non-performance poet of the twenty-first century, whether fifteen or sixty years old, from Zimbabwe, New York or Leeds, begin the difficult quest for readership? Resources for publication have never been so numerous. Small presses dedicated to poetry continue to be born. Radio and television experiment with new ways of presenting verse. The culture of independent little magazines is vigorous, the reading circuit much travelled. There is, too, that greatest resource, the Internet, where poetry is posted, exchanged and commented upon. Virtual workshops and magazines abound.

And yet it has never been more difficult for a poet to find a literal, earth-bound readership. The culture of reception is not so much unwelcoming as blasé. If there isn't a handle, a 'symbol of security' to recommend a new author (youth, political or other differentiation), editors are inclined to say that 'it isn't likely to be of interest to our readers'. Mere excellence has never been more mere. Readers are incurious about the art of poetry and its continuities. The roots of our general reading culture trail back little further than the nineteenth century. The eighteenth is almost wholly aban-doned. There may be day-tours to pre-Restoration times, but no one stays overnight. Everyone has a favourite, Wyatt or Herbert or Clare, but a limited sense of their context. The misvaluing of contemporary poetry begins in a willed ignorance of where the vigour and – to use Seamus Heaney's term – *redress* of poetry come from. *Why* are Donne's stanzas found wanting and awkward by Ben Jonson, why are Dr Johnson and T.S. Eliot so impatient of Milton, why is Wordsworth's revolution in diction so radical, how does Whitman fit into the picture of Modernism? Poetry as a language of argument, exploration, synthesis? Such notions belong to the academy and in its obscurer and more demanding forms to a dank, fennish corner of it.

An interest in how poems work is a form of tenured pedantry. Artifice gets in the way of the expression of true feeling. But the expression of true feeling is not quite the same thing as the true expression of feeling. A poet careless of technique, of diction and syntax to begin with, may pour forth real feeling, but the language will not convey that feeling. The language many take to be poetic is as ready-made as the fridge-magnet phrases that entertain bored children and adults waiting for supper. Each day, somewhere in an Anglophone country, a would-be poet amazes himself by discovering – metaphor! Or finds herself putting words with a similar sound at the ends of consecutive lines and look, she has happened upon rhyme.

This, like *New Poetries I* and *II*, is a multicultural anthology. Writers from Africa, America and Europe are included, each from a different background and spanning four generations. What do the twelve poets included have in common? Though they are all able to perform their poems in public and do it well, none is a performance poet. Each is formally curious, though the formal directions they take are quite distinct. They write to explore language and subject matter, sometimes to re-evoke (not remember), sometimes to fix down a paradox or an irony, sometimes to see in new ways. The poems do not seem to me, for the most part, to have been written simply to entertain. That they do so, that they are by turns funny and moving, wry and savage, is proof of the power of engagement with real subjects and forms that each poet has achieved.

MICHAEL SCHMIDT

Caroline Bird

CAROLINE BIRD was born in London in 1986. She has lived in Leeds for most of her life, attending the York Steiner School. She now lives in South London and goes to Eleanor Holles School, where she is studying for her GCSEs. She has been a winner of the Simon Elvin Young Poet of the Year Awards in 1999 and 2000, she was shortlisted for the Geoffrey Dearmer Prize 2000 and is on the shortlist for the Eric Gregory Awards, 2002. Her first collection, *Looking Through Letterboxes*, was published in February 2002.

Of the poems in this selection, 'Gingerbread House' was first published in *PN Review* and 'Suddenly I was Hilarious' was first published in *The North*.

Badger Watching

Badger watching wasn't my first choice,
or my second either, but here we are, face down
like playing cards on the brink of a hill.
Stars and molehills, waiting for the badgers.

We'd painted our faces, unravelled
down the lane before the cold could track us down.
But now, now that your voice is seeping into my pores
and the badgers have stood us up, left us at the altar

with a tuft of grass and a tree, it's tempting,
tempting to tilt sideways and leave you behind,
roll hips first down badger mountain
into the blue green belly of the lake.

After two hours we will leave, avoiding the path
because we prefer to trip up, but pretending,
behind our foreheads, that we could have seen badgers.
Maybe, if we'd enticed them out with sausages.

No One in the Waiting Room Looks Up

A power-ranger child runs up the wall. Which wall?
The white wall, the one which gives you a coma

if you stare for too long. The child doesn't come down,
ate so much chocolate from the vending machines,

he's learnt how to fly. But no one in the waiting room looks up.
Christmas is coming and Santa Claus is in Ward 17,

turn left at the end of the corridor. A woman with a pick-axe
is strolling past the operation room, looking for someone to whack.

A prune-faced man is spray-painting obscenities
up and down the hall and a dressing-gown awash in antiseptic

swaggers around the hospital, proud of its bodylessness.
A patient in a wheelbarrow is sped across the corridor,

choking to death on a grape – though of course they will say
he choked until he was un-alive, but not dead,

because people don't die. Not even the lad who's still up the wall,
which wall? The white wall. But no one in the waiting room looks up.

The Radiator in Your Room

I'm thinking of the radiator in your room.
I'm thinking of all your knife-in-the-dark remarks,
of the way you fold yourself into bed like a fig-roll
and blow out the lights with the breath of a switch.

I'm fast forwarding through swirling colours
and tilting handshakes, an agreement sealed by a word,
only a word, only a cheek tongue cough
that came out wrong. I'm rewinding
all my dreams, the way they flow
like a tap of steaming memories through a sieve
of boiling red lights on your digital alarm clock.
I'm pausing flashbacks and printing them out:
they smell of ink and freshly cut trees,
they smell of mornings, lying with my back
to the ceiling, my cooling dreams a puddle on the floor.

I'm thinking of rain drawn back up the ladder
of your tree-house and into the sky, making you
younger by a few seconds. I'm thinking of babies
drinking from troughs of milk, being pigs for a day
and builders with muscles like radishes,
breaking their backs on the final brick.

Before the Story Goes

Finally I turned around in the plastic seat,
make-up flaking in the moonlight, to look
until you stopped making sense.
You were writing my name in the air
with your snub nose, injecting your mouth
with gum from a pink packet.
I watched the thought bubbles stretch
and blow themselves up. Funny,
how the night sometimes freezes,
poises me in one of those statue modes,
where however much I try, I can't raise my head.
And so, before the morning when the story goes,
we sat, you and I, on the verge of hating.
Your eyes level with the window, mine
with the crack in the door, becoming smaller
with every flicker of a breath.

Playing at Families

When you can pick up your mother in thickset hands,
roll her over and tenderly remove her wings.

When you can rip off your father's moustache
with a twitch of finger and thumb,

telling him, 'It'll never do good with the ladies,
not any more.'

When you can place them on your shelf,
like miniature models, knowing that every night

they search the bedroom,
looking for lovers and empty wine bottles,

but melt into the carpet when you open your eyes.
When you can arrange your grandparents in tiny velvet chairs

and gently put them in the embers of the fire,
soothing them through cooing lips

that you're 'Well fed and educated,' so there's no need to worry.
When you can put your relatives in separate boxes

to make sure they don't breed or cut each other's hair
while you're out of the house.

When you can lift them, light as a feather, kiss them
and tuck them in matchbox beds,

making sure your family are locked in innocent slumber,
before leaving to go clubbing every night.

When you can do all this, then you have to face the guilt
when finally, after too many years, you creep back in

to find each wide awake and crying
that they hadn't known where you were.

Suddenly I was Hilarious

Even the rain was throwing back its head.
I never knew I was so funny. They were pulling out their hair
in clumps and stuffing it in their mouths, they were sitting
on window-sills and falling out of windows.
I can't quite remember how it started,
maybe when the bedclothes tittered as I headed for the sink
and the toothbrush chattered on my teeth.

When I reached the foot of the stairs,
the girl with the ponytail choked on her own tongue
and the man with the face like a paving slab cracked up.
Suddenly I was hilarious. I was perched cross-legged on the sofa,
the sky collapsing down into the drains,
I had everyone from the neighbourhood gathered
around my ankles, bursting.
I had them all in stitches just by twitching my eye.

But the rain stopped at midnight.

By this time their throats were bleeding
and helicopters had sifted people in from around the globe,
just to catch a glimpse.
But when the rain died there was silence.
Then shaking of heads,
and the stepping back into of planes.
After, it was kind of a shock
when I placed a mug on the table and nobody laughed.

I Know this Because You Told Me

I'll break my neck if I jump again from the top of these stairs.
I'll suffer for the rest of my life in hospital
if I put my finger up my nose and then the wind changes.
I know this because you told me.

I'll drown if I jump once more in this nice muddy puddle,
there'll be a flash flood and the rain will rise and take us all.
The world should live in perfect harmony
and you'll kill the bloody neighbours if they don't trim their hedge.

I should never swear, I know this because you told me.
If I talk to the teachers about our mortgage and the fact
that we don't pay our bills, then a monster will come out of the toilet
in the dead of night and pull me down.

You are not joking and only want to warn me. You are a good parent
and tell me life as it is, I know this because you told me.
If I fall in love at seventeen then it will not last.
If I eat too much I will explode and muck up your new shirt.

If I burp then I will blow myself inside out. The world
is quite a strange place and everyone is strange except you.
I know this because you told me.
If I take money from your wallet it is called crime,

if you take money from my piggy bank it is called borrowing.
If I never have a bath I will smell and people won't walk
on the same side of the street as me,
but if I do then I'll be sucked down the plug hole. Some women shave.

I know this because you told me. The banister is for holding,
not for sliding down and you were never rude to your parents.
I'll break my neck if I jump again from the top of these stairs
and no, I should not do it anyway.

Gingerbread House

He smelt of 'fresh from the oven' adulthood,
his tongue on the hinge of his lips, his eyes spinning
with sex and cinnamon as he invited you in.
You gazed with wonder at his gingerbread house,
rocking back on your heels with childish delight.
You took a long drag on your lollypop stick
then flicked it away.
Later you spat it all back out to your friends,
showed them the goodies you'd brought back
hidden underneath your tongue. You licked
their pink bedrooms with your knowledge,
spread your laughter thumb-deep on their walls,
tasted the irony on your teeth.

Look little children, come peek at the trail of bread,
look how the teeth marks are still fresh
since they were ripped from the loaf,
look how the birds swoop, hundreds and thousands
of hungry red mouths.

Liquorice doormat, sherbet-coated window pane,
marzipan-stained glass, milk chocolate letterbox,
gingerbread door. His hair like spun sugar
in your hands.
More cream in your coffee dear?
You really are the sweetest child.

Running through the forest, the soft breeze
at each girl's back, like the sound of fairies' wings.
Swooping, diving, disappearing in the shadows,
they come like wolves to the house where he sleeps.
The wizard, the prince, the eldest son
and as his walls are eaten from around his bed,
he dreams of adult things, running, swooping,
diving and of how the sugar doesn't taste as sweet
once you've gorged, indulged, stuffed yourself
with every crumb, every lick and strip.
Left not a single melting piece untouched.

He smelt of 'fresh from the oven' adulthood
They eat him too, his pale skin vibrates in their fingers,
and the rain falls on his mattress and the place
where his house used to be.

At last, licking their lips they return to the forest,
no longer wolves, just girls. They look for their path
through the night. Lost. They blame the Robins,
they blame the Swallows, they blame the Swans,
the Eagles, they blame the Vultures
and their hungry red mouths.

My Love

I like you best when you're not here, my love.
Flowers are colourful knives, smiles, frowns
plastered in foundation, blaming eyes simply
pools of affection. My love. Don't relax, don't sit back.
The ghosts who have finished their business,
but hang around purely for fun, rustle the curtains
in the morning and put salt in my mouth as I sleep.
I wake with grains of hate on my tongue.
My love, for you are the source of the winding
sewers, the bursting balloon pumped with spite
that shatters into the sky. If I throw you off
it will rise even higher, darling. Outside car doors
are slamming, alarms are being triggered, people
run like blurs across blank pages that are soon
to be filled. I like you best when you're not here,
my love. No, I won't get up, you can let yourself out.

Linda Chase

LINDA CHASE was born in New Jersey in 1941 and grew up in Manhasset, Long Island. She did an undergraduate degree in creative writing at Bennington College in Vermont and then moved to San Francisco where she worked as a stage costume designer.

In 1968 she moved to Scotland, where her children were born. She began her lifelong study of tai chi and continued to work in theatre and community arts in Edinburgh. She now lives in Manchester where she writes and studies poetry and also teaches tai chi.

Her books include *Young Men Dancing* (pamphlet by Smith/Doorstop), *These Goodbyes* (Fatchance Press) and *The Wedding Spy* (Carcanet). Of the poems in this anthology, 'Cut Fruit', 'Night Vision', 'Big Blue Sofas', 'The Dinner Kiss' and 'Daily Practice' first appeared in *The Wedding Spy*.

Cut Fruit

Cutting fruit for you
as early and as quietly as I could,
I chose the only white plate there was
and laid the fruit out like a star.

I couldn't rest the plate on your back
in case you moved and tipped it,
so I held it above your left shoulder,
without moving, until you woke.

You pick a crescent slice of peach
and slip the juicy surfaces between your lips.
At once my tongue aches, my mouth floods.
I know I could suck the taste out of you.

Perhaps I'll have to get up earlier
and cut the pieces finer.
Dawn slides in an instant
and the juices have run in the plate.

Night Vision

The bed is piled high with white.
All six plumped up pillows are white
and the night shirt I have on is white
and the lampshade and the blinds are white
and the rugs around the bed are white
and I wait here, covered, while you wash.
Then you come dripping, rubbing your rump
buffing your back, trailing the towel
and I open the duvet and draw you in
as the feathers fill their cases, freshness

from the bath, gardenia scent from the soap,
making much lighter the white in the room.
You tell me it's time to go to sleep,
but sleep is for people blinded by dark.

Big Blue Sofas

The big blue sofas are coming
early in the morning. We've cleared
everything out of the room
and made enough space in the hall.

                    You've had to tell me everything
                      quickly, before the doorbell rings.
              When I felt your arm around me, I woke
                 to hear you say, 'My god, five bottles.'

The sofas are dark blue – navy, almost –
and one of them is as long as the wall.
The other one seats three people who agree
to sit up straight, or one person who sprawls.

                    You gather my breast from where
                        it has slid down along my ribcage
                  and then you find the nipple easily.
                    Some men have a knack for this.

The longer sofa seats four, which could be
three children and about two cats.
Not white cats, of course. Not white on navy,
though the people can wear whatever they like.

Even while gently scooping my breast
you talk about cocaine and smoking draw
and matted memories of greedy sex
as if I could absolve you, clear your slate.

The sofas will be set at right angles
to each other with a low table in between
on which everyone from both sofas can put
their feet and their remote controls.

I slide my hand down your back
further than most daytime friends might,
even though all night I had been careful
not to slip that hand between your legs.

One person will have to walk backwards,
I imagine, and the other one won't.
The cushions might still be wrapped
separately in thick milky polythene bags.

I want to love you on a new day,
clearly, using everything I've got
and I want to sit at right angles to the walls
and flip through every channel.

I can hardly wait for the doorbell to ring.
I want furniture to be carried down the hall.
I want big blue sofas and kids and cats
and cushions and perfect reception on the bloody TV.

The Dinner Kiss

The cooking had been a chore –
the knives not sharp enough,
no overall menu planned in my head
and the guests had not been counted.

Yet somehow everyone fitted in –
the Scots, big and boisterous, squeezed
beside the buttoned-up Japanese
while the Americans brought in chairs.

Vegetables could have been the cause,
finally, of the seating plan's collapse.
The garlic scented potatoes with herbs
made everyone stand to help themselves.

I thought you were heading for the fridge
when you got up, the way an old friend can,
cool as you like, making mince meat
of the demure Japanese manners.

Maybe a can of beer or ketchup, I thought.
Just one of those sudden mid-meal needs.
And to tell the truth, there is nothing
I would have kept from you.

So, when you walked around the table
and lifted me out of my seat
as if your mouth had done it alone
without the help of your arms,

I rose, a stringless helium balloon,
so light, hovering over the table,
I thought I would never stop rising,
not ever, and then the kiss began.

Daily Practice

Was it you who made the tea in the yellow pot
and lit the Chinese incense before I came downstairs?
You and fresh flowers, arranged in front of me.

We sit cross-legged through this unfolding hour,
held by long, sweet in-breaths before the traffic stirs,
stopping and starting our minds with lists of things to do.

All day we vie with our computers, scanners, phones
and bounce around within our carnival of screens
reading messages – these tiny bits of text that bind.

You mustn't tell anyone I've cooked for you tonight.
These are secret bowls of food we eat with chop-sticks
behind the jasmine trellis when the sun goes down.

Come here. Our final practice time is in the dark.
I find you by touch and stick to you all night,
though I know you don't know how dark it can get.

You could have been surprised by this waking up,
not knowing where in the world this new place is.
It is black and blacker. It is light and lighter.

Restaurant

People are eating and passing food across this table
upon which you have immobilised my right hand
against the wood with your own firm left hand.

Everyone can see that you have got me
anchored in place, your hobbled left-handed lover
still able to eat, but not to wander off.

There is no struggle whatsoever to be seen.
Not a finger of mine slips through any of yours
as part of a cunning strategy for escape.

Tamed and tethered, I graze contentedly
in front of the very friends who think me wild.
It excites them. In their dreams you pin me down.

Red Wings

Your long red-shirted arms flailed
like giant crane wings on the balcony
as if they would lift and let you glide over
Kentish Town and further north to Hampstead.

I would hitch a ride on your back,
brave as Amelia Erhart with goggles
looking down on London, waiting
until we saw the trees and ponds of the Heath.

Then you could land on a sloping meadow
and wrap me in those long red arms
and we'll roll together down into a thicket,
tumbled, entwined around each other.

It was just a bit of dancing on the balcony
as the sun sank through the pink sky
and you got so carried away. And I?
I went every bit of the distance with you.

My Brave Pink

My brave pink/purple, front-line heart
(a proper little cliff-hanger with wings,
parachute and fitted on-impact airbags)
is on the ground in smithereens.

Too high up for the safety valve to open
and too quick falling to unfold the wings.
Airbags might as well have been rocks,
once the bottom had been hit.

Don't bother to scrape it up
or reshape it into some two-bit valentine.
I don't want lace, ribbons or a message.
Show mercy. Leave it blank.

Passing the Parcel

Passing the parcel back and forth between us,
dropping tears on the delicate tissue paper,
and crushing the ribbon with our sweaty hands,
has made the package nearly unrecognisable.

It might be a stage prop from a Christmas pantomime,
thrown from actor to actor in spurts, manhandled,
while the audience shouts, 'He's behind you!'
'Throw it!' so I look around, but you aren't.

It rattles like a nest of boxes, one inside the other
carefully disguised to look like something nice
which I could then hand to a friend, smiling.
Perhaps expensive chocolates are inside.

But I remember well what's in the inner box.
Why else would I be trying so hard to give it back?
It wasn't meant for me. It wasn't meant for me.
You are thinking to yourself exactly the same thing.

Passing the parcel back and forth between us,
we watch the soggy wrappings drop away,
we see the matted ribbon undo itself like salty rope.
Believe me, there is no mistake boxed inside these boxes.

Last Logging On

It's a Friday kind of thing
between signing off and signing on –
leaving the office and going home.

Do I mind that you think of me –
that you send me a message saying
I am beautiful?

The word beautiful makes me close my eyes
to remember what it was like. I can't imagine
who has sent this message, nor to whom,

though I know these people well
when they have nothing to say,
Monday to Thursday.

Swithun Cooper

SWITHUN COOPER was born in 1983 and grew up in Reading. He was a winner in the Simon Elvin Young Poet of the Year Awards 2000, as well as the Peterloo Poets Competition and the Christopher Tower Poetry Prizes in 2001. He is currently studying English Literature and Creative Writing at Warwick University.

Road Rage

She left him on the A329M.
She tried to break the bad news to him gently –
From this point on, there would be no more them.

She tried to break her bad news to him gently
Until she heard him go off on a bender
And roar: *Beat back that bitch in her black Bentley!*

Fuck up her forty-five pound foreign fender!
From *this* point on, there would be no more them
His sanity had been returned to sender.

She left him on the A329M;
She motored through her speech, driven by fear
And, heavily, she slammed the brakes on. Then

She clutched at her opinions. *You, my dear,*
Let road rage rampage through you permanently.
We can't go on, unless we both change gear

And maybe steer ourselves intelligently.
From this point on, there would be no more them,
And he broke down – she'd *tried* to do it gently.

Violet

I would suggest your aura could get lost,
But there is only one place it can fit
(And surgically removing it would cost).
I would suggest your aura could get lost,
Or buffed up nicely, plated or embossed:
Think of a way to make me stomach it.
I would suggest your aura could get lost,
But there is only one place it can fit.

Drinking the Thames through a Straw

I am drinking the Thames through a straw.
I've been doing it most of the day,
Though I'd never have done it before

I met you. I've gone out of my way
(Getting waterweed clogged in my teeth)
Just imagining what you might say

If I turned up with flowers beneath
Your small window, with oil-slick breath
And three ducks and a boat in my teeth.

Would you tell me you'd rather date death?
Does this sacrifice need something more
For a person who's seemingly sore
While I'm drinking the Thames through a straw?

Songs by The Smiths

Disrupted moments never can remember
What they were, or they thought they were, before.
Just like the smoke forgets the dying ember,
Filling forgets its tooth, wall forgets floor,
You cannot recollect six months' existence
Because you spent it all checking the distance
Between what you had and what you were looking for.

What we appreciate, we've left behind us.
What's useful, though, we relegate and smother
For fear of what we've found coming to find us:
We took for granted significant other
Surroundings: we had seats yet chose to stand.
A secret treaty passes second-hand,
The sleeping child is envied by the sleepless mother.

I'm glad we went astray, but think we might
Have stood a chance when lost among the piths.
When going wrong, you really must go wrong *right*
And gain a record with the urban myths.
This is how I would have liked us to end:
At the party of someone else's friend,
Free alcohol, free cigarettes, songs by The Smiths.

Welcome to the end of our scarlet letter.
Though we dried up, we could have dried up better.

Oeuvre and Out

His glasses bend through their Sellotape wrap,
He claims to hate computers, writes by hand,
Gets zeitgeist, like his beer, straight from the tap,
On Friday nights he's bassist for a band,

By day he's drunk and so he works by night,
His inspiration's buy one get one free,
Gets genius direct on satellite
And in the adverts, watching ITV,

He scribbles in a ring-bound, A5 pad,
His metaphors are cosy, trite and warm,
He spent his gap year dealing in Baghdad,
Gets motivation from a tax-rate form,

He eschews rhythm, writes poems of sound,
He'll kill himself and end up world-renowned.

Severe Weather

The sun, so hot it melts itself away,
Drips rays of liquid light into the room
And wraps around my tongue for half the day
Like molten velvet, rinsed through old perfume.

★

The air is soft and thick with promised rain.
I'm walking through a street of see-through mist,
But sharing its humidity again
Feels less like breathing, more like being kissed.

★

This fog's a breathy secret in the mouth
Which creeps from nostrils, settles in the lungs.
It travels through the blood from North to South
And sits, expanded warmth, like tips of tongues.

★

A powder-compact residue returns
Then crumbles, whether left behind or taken.
So anyone caught in the storm soon learns
That closed-in worlds can be held up and shaken.

★

A steady change is going on in here –
Nothing has been replaced, instead it's grown.
I know that it will all seem less severe
Whether or not I make my feelings known.

Don't Dress Down

He walks into the room, a goldfish bowl
Instead of what we'd like to call a head,
His childhood sweetheart now decked in a shoal
With minnows swarming over her instead.
The woman to the left of me stands up,
Recites a bidding prayer, sits down, retreats
Into her small-talk bible. *Raise a cup
To old friends, new friends, friends!* We take our seats.

Two old friends, but too old, friends. No release –
Unless one of her minnows takes his bait.
If demons feed themselves on half-cooked peace,
Right now, they're spoiled for choice and overweight.
But unlike them, she looks a little thinner:
No, really, darling, don't dress down for dinner.

Not an Important Failure

Her patchwork hands, stitched up to suit his fingers,
Straighten her shortened skirt eternally.
A scent of desperation kind of lingers
Round her, although she says it's CK Be.

In someone else's bed she paints a picture
Across the perfect sheets. She's in a state.
Her art releases a disturbing mixture
Of truth and dream. They do not correlate.

Meanwhile, he's stepping over cracks in pavements.
He'd break her in if she were just a shoe.
Their conversation is awash with statements
With each one drowning in the other's view.

The china doll still copies her expression
But its appearance fades from too much light.
She keeps her own in shadows, a confession
She's yet to tell him outside of the night.

He'd walk all over her if she had cracks in.
She's getting sick of being his right hand.
What they want most, their partnership still lacks in
But that's something they'll never understand.

Autumnesque

Now that each leaf has come to understand
That winter is a giving, not a stealing,
In terms of time
Internal rhyme
Is hardly what you'd want to call appealing.
Who'd rhyme in the middle? Better the end,
They think. And so they journey towards land.

A problem then emerges in the falling –
Is landing slow and soft, or hard and fast?
Like treading water
In bricks and mortar
The problem stays, suspended and uncast.
The problem is enticing yet appalling;
The problem comes from speeding up and stalling.

The young leaves do not know what falling's for.
The old ones know that summer is bereft,
So from their care
A gnarled and bare
Stump is abandoned, cold and grey and left.
Experience can teach them so much more,
Why rich and green must turn to brown and poor.

Alone, I notice, sitting at my desk,
At some point each of us is autumnesque.

The Princess in the Tower-Block

Through concrete, plastic, glassware and cement
Surroundings, she succeeded, caught his eye –
Through hard-boiled egos, she picked up the scent:
Her hero in a matching suit and tie.

For lack of spinning wheel, she pricked her thumb
Whilst cutting up an information sheet.
She waited, nine to five, for him to come
And with bravura, sweep her off her feet.

He'd slain the beast of corporate companies
And stained his sword with blood of marketeers.
He'd brought the Software Demons to their knees
And earned a fortune that would last for years.

He'd bought for her (not fought for her) a ring.
They rode into the sunset, full of laughter,
Not on a horse: a bus to Kettering.
They lived – some say – happily ever after.

Julie Crane

Julie Crane was born in Worcester in 1962, and was educated there and at Durham, where she now lives and teaches in the university. She is married, with two daughters.

The Accident

'Mike and Claire are shagging. Better not
disturb them, Vince – hand me the keys. I'll drive.'
No sooner said. Keith drove. But because
he'd always had a thing for Claire
he took a corner sharp, and suddenly
he saw an angel, looking down at him,
tut-tutting, but pleased to see him anyway,
like his own mum when he came in late.

He only knew for certain he was dead
when she pointed out to him his own limp form
covered over, given up on, while they tried to haul
Vince out of the wreckage. Then Claire and Mike turned up,
Uncoupled, and it was his name, Keith was glad to see,
that she screamed out first. Then the Saturday night angel
twitched a bit, and said, 'best leave them to it,'
so he did. He had to. Story of his life.

Afterwards, Mike didn't hang around long. What with
the fuss in the papers, Vince hanging on,
and Claire's litmus paper turning pink, he thought
'I've had it with this town,' and scarpered,
down South somewhere, nobody knew. Come June,
the flowers they spread for the dead boy
just at the spot where the midnight angel loomed
looked jaded and bereft. But Claire felt better,
pushing her baby with her figure back,
counting her blessings in the summer air –
Mike gone (no loss, that one – everybody said);
Keith dead and buried – nothing to be done;
Vince coming round most evenings – baby fine.
'We should've called you Lucky, kid,' she said.

Reading *Jane Eyre* with my Daughters

I explain, after the first paragraph,
that walks were different, winters different,
houses and cousins differently arranged.
We brush past the differences, the parentheses,
the early dining, the Victorian orphan state,
and soon we are in the raw specialness
of childhood, where no explanations
are needed.

It is time to be done with reverence.
They were ill and poor, and one should say so,
and be done with it, the sad governesses,
the cramped rooms and girlish loves, the tiny dresses
which we touch with wonder and dismay,
not for the tiny frames, but for the starved hearts
which chafed in them. And beyond it all
the tilting, waiting churchyard, the sad
and desperate sisters in their patient home,
the sitting-room paced, the moors
ransacked for stories.

Even as I say, 'I could take you there,'
I know that even if the gloom obliges,
the 'no possibility' of weather
will be suggestive only. You, with your brighter prospect,
will not associate their sisterhood
with yours, for their world
has no need to be grasped by you, nor the meaning
of their peculiar sadness, as sister
after sister faded, until only
the invented world of childhood, and
the curious, uneven novels remained.

And take you where?
They mapped a landscape out, and its mode
was interior and passionate, and it has nothing to say
except sorrow. It does not live
in the narrow dresses, silent moors,
in the constantly visited and empty house.

It lies here, in this first chapter,
and in your listening consciousness, where you wait
for the child in the window-seat, locked in,
locked out, to narrate her story,
which you receive with your indifferent grace.

Leaving France

Since our compact is ending, and since I understand
that to enter a different language is to say
farewell to self and home, and to become
a desperate character, I know that the next time
I see you will be in the intangible
shape of memory: you will have become
the exile, innocent and dream-like,
while I stand on firm land again. Meanwhile,
'goodbye', say the children, goodbye
les ânes, goodbye les chats, goodbye La Loge
where the small irritations of language
are already fading: twenty minutes will see to it,
shake you like a parasol, and what remains
will be the suddenness of difference – houses solid, trees
whose formidable green gives sure commands:
this is your country: you must speak in it.

Meeting Margaret Tyson, 1592

First, pare down all meaning. If you meet
It must be on her terms. Notice the landscape –
Even name the flowers – oxslip, hyssop, may –
But don't dare to translate it. The things that you have read
Let them stay pocketed – she has not read them, seen them.

Do not say, even, loving the running gold,
The green, the lingering cusp of evening,
'You have such consolations.' Her century's terrors
Are nothing to her, and its beauty is the dower
She takes for granted. Her father's house

Beyond her, she is beyond your reach,
Intelligent but not contemplative, even her beauty
Austere, unknowable. The man she waits for
Is not her own, it is her sister's squire,
She is a sister merely, waiting. Look,

There is no passion in her glance: do not suppose it.
History, when it is felt, must work like this,
Like meditation. If you see, in the long furl
Of shadows gathering, her own headstone,
With that name on that she can barely manage,

Do not suppose she cannot sense its coming,
Or turn to greet it calmly, though a girl.

The Old Reign

One must have been born
in the old reign
to feel the distress
of mid-century,

one must have seen
the yellow fields,
the tall
headdresses;

or the girl from Spain
riding through town
on her way to be queen,
the hem of her gown

no longer turned
by her own hand
till twenty summers
had seen her fade;

one must have been stirred
by the lyrical call
of the ballads they made
they will never sing for you;

and know that memory is gone,
horror prodigal;
that your doom is mid-century,
and the old reign is done.

Elegy for a Literary Plotter

Sarky, your day is over!
With your taut passion and your pet
Hates, and the lost love
We invented for you, have you ever
Made it through the sixty-sixth sonnet
Without crying yet?

Who will comfort youth with sadness now?
'We must eat, as the Russian says,
Today, or at least tomorrow,
And so Sorrow
Loses Sway.'

Sorrow, your poet's 'deceiving elf',
With her wings like ravens and her eyes like diamond
Forever brooding over English Literature
Scattering griefs in far-flung counties
Over poetry and the rich,

'And those whose hold on the substantial
Was tenuous, like poor John Keats
And Hamlet the Dane and,
If I am not very much deceived, myself'

Your counties and your shires:
Your voice divided England for us.
You had the Woodhouses and the Darcys
And the Feverels in their places, and remarked,
Of Lady Dedlock and of Hallam, 'you will find
That every time Literature visits Lincolnshire, it is raining.'

For years I have forgotten you, until today
Far in the North where churlish earls conspired
For hands of queens,
And nowhere near to Chesney Wold,
The rain against this terrace tap tap taps once more
Your harrowing tales out; your rhetoric and mood
Again possess the world; and then, by the late post,
From legion sleeping shires away
And stained by half a kingdom's gales – this news, this news.

Last Words

Our last words will matter.
They will cast their shade
longer than attitude.

You cannot practise them.
Though men have brought the block
at your request

for you to lay your head on,
no readiness
can spur words on,

for they will be alert
to anything that happens:
a cough, a tear,

a bird in flight.
Your gown will twitch, and you
will be altered

impeccably, forever.
Beyond our tragedy, do you not hear
the stir, the sigh of words?

One Hit Wonder

And so, because of the helpless levelling-out of lives,
And because the hall is silenced
Where you were a teenage legend,
And books close round me now like sentinels
Confounding the old adventures,
I would like – before I am thirty, say –
To compose the one-hit-wonder
That stirs a generation for a summer.

Imagine the scenarios: the honeysuckle
By the open doorway,
The serious conversations on the scented lawns,
And suddenly, with a careless intervention,
The familiar chords come stealing.

And radios on beaches! The coastal towns
Alive with the melody;
Someone always feeding coins into a juke-box
Like a church donation, so as to receive once more
Its casual radiant promise;

And striking up the old chords decades later
When, hearing it again,
You are longing for the juke-boxes, the beaches,
Your love as it was then.

My Father's House

In my father's house the years stretched out
Like rolling hay, like acres, a sure land.
No one came and no one went
That would make a dog's nose twitch. Marriages were made,
Deaths were tolled, and liveries were worn. It was well-known
How someone once had been
Raised on the field of battle – Bosworth, was it? – and so
Started it all off – the cunning, loyal men,

The faithful wives and servants, the good harvests,
The good silk, visits, gifts that must
Be noted, daughters heavy with brocade.
Cradles rocked adeptly, knowing
Their place in the world, features were passed on
Complacently, knowing the figure they must make.
But every lineage has its moment
Of pure fracture, the known form
Is shaken, the mint
Cannot hammer away forever, pure cheek,
Blue eye, and for my father's house
The change was unremarkable, but final:
I was born.

Ben Downing

BEN DOWNING was born in Massachusetts in 1967 and graduated from Harvard in 1989. He lives in New York City with his wife and daughter, and is the managing editor of *Parnassus*. His poems, essays, and reviews have been published in *PN Review*, *The Atlantic Monthly*, *The New Criterion*, *The Wall Street Journal*, *The New York Times Book Review*, *The Yale Review*, and elsewhere.

Saudades

is what my student said he'd feel for me
upon returning to Brazil, and how
he felt right then, in fact, about the place
he'd left behind. He spoke the word as if
it were the loneliest, most dignified
sound that human tongues had ever wrapped
themselves around, his face aflame with that
peculiar pride in the untranslatable.
But still we tried to find some semblance
of an English shape: a pining when applied
to absent people, or homesickness
where the land's at stake. And although I
– who had no Portuguese – could only take
from him a faint, imperfect imprint, I press
it here for you to see, knowing as I do
that *love* in any language comes out clear.

Inshallah

– which is to say 'God willing', more or less:
a phrase that rose routinely to her lips
whenever plans were hatched or hopes expressed,
the way we knock on wood, yet fervently,
as if to wax too confident might be
to kill the very thing she wanted most.

It used to pique and trouble me somehow,
this precautionary tic of hers, but now
I understand why she was sceptical
of what Allah in His caprice allots,
because that she should live He did not will,
or, more terribly, He did that she should not.

i.m. Mirel Sayinsoy 1967–1999

One Green Stone

*... celui qui trouve son emploi dans
la contemplation d'une pierre verte...*
St-John Perse

He who finds his business in the slow,
persistent study of one green stone,
even a plain one chosen, let us say,
from a plenitude of greater green;

and who, in choosing green, abandons blue
to its own scholar, snubs all reds, rejects
the dark persuasions of persistent black;
and whose choice of stone as well reflects

the surface of a world neglected – not
without pain, but without regret – of things
crying out their equal worth, their need
to have their facets noted, diamond rings

and the humblest wooden chair alike
in the futile clamour of the claims they make
upon the student who, studying his one
green stone, considers that, and that alone.

The Mixer

Our moods do not believe in each other.
Emerson

How true. And so, having vowed to introduce
my sceptical own, I planned a splashy fête,
then worked through my black book's alphabet:
Abjection, Humdrum, Mr Perky, Zeus

(as Drug-Fuelled Cockiness styles himself these days)
were all pressed warmly to my posh soirée.
The whole thing went swimmingly – at first.
Impatience huffed in early, fretted, cursed

the tardy guests, but settled down when Mellow
administered shiatsu. The same
effect was had by Thoughts of Long Ago
on Dwelling in the Future: each became

the other's palliating complement;
a jolly pair they made, equivalent
together to Atop the Moment's Wave,
who had begged off. Lookin' to Misbehave

ducked sheepishly back into line when faced
with the righteous mug of Good Samaritan;
Glad hugged Sad; Mad took a pill. But then,
when Bumptious Dickhead started to lambast

the Soul of Thoughtfulness, the atmosphere
queasily curdled and reversed itself.
The Four Humours came as one, snickered, jeered
the junior metaphors; Rude Aerobic Health

leapt to their defence; Atrabile got spilled;
Choleric oozed across the floor and kindled
High Dudgeon, who'd been stewing in his chair,
abruptly into Rabid. Everywhere,

it seemed, a mood now trounced its opposite,
behaviours with their loathed antipodes
squared violently off: What Will Be
Will Be and Seize Control of Your Own Fate,

Hunkydory pistolwhipped by Fuck the World,
Thin-skinned v. Unflappable, Sourpuss
contending Chipper, Genteel with Churl,
fisticuffs 'twixt Tightwad and Magnanimous,

Kinky humping Prude, Laodicean
by Zealot gruesomely crucified,
with Hamlet, Pangloss, Calvin with Wilde,
the Draco in me punishing the King,

and all, of course, ganging up on Paranoid;
not even Blah quite managed to avoid
the brutal fray of temperaments.
Eventually the warring parties spent

themselves, desisted grudgingly, and left,
each to his remote sarcophagus.
I paused. And next, both Relieved and Bereft
(loyal chums, they'd stayed behind), began to suss

my curious situation out. They'd met,
irrefutably, and fought, loved, swived,
abominated, swapped gossip of my lives,
snubbed, empathised, flouted Etiquette.

The raucous proof was iron-clad, I thought:
those phantoms at whose substance they'd once scoffed
had been made real for them far past dispute.
No longer could they hoist their haughty snoots

disdainfully above their brethren;
besides, I mused, they have in common *me*.
Isn't that enough? You'd think they'd want to bend
their passions to my central peace, agree

on some hybrid, ideal specimen,
neither Grim nor falsely Debonair,
not Tart, not Saccharine, but measured, fair,
and sleekly fitted to the subtle end

of animal satiety. Alas.
So little's changed. My selves go blithely on
as if they'd never butted heads or razzed
their Manichaean twins, as if beyond

their meagre pale lived only reprobates
instead of what I'd shown: valid traits
clobbering yet buttressing their own –
quel paradoxe. Each still swears that he alone

exists, has claim to me, is singular,
supreme, nonrelative, and permanent.
And who am I to doubt such wisdom when
I am the Bittersweet whose sum they are?

Prothalamion
for Michele

The *cleaving* properties of love
(in both conflicting senses of

that Freud-deflowered word: to split
violently; bindingly to knit)

are such that every one becomes,
by action of its medium,

      either halved or magnified.
      While the harder meaning I'd

more often met with in the past –
the sundered pride, the heart crevassed –

its stronger valence now cements
those parts of me that had been rent,

and melds them with your own bits till
we're alloyed in love's crucible.

Aeolian Kazoo

Not the dulcet harp of Thomson, Coleridge,
et al. I can't afford the ormolu,
the pretence of the wind god whiffling through
in celestial puffs, a kapellmeister midge

at work for me, pluck pluck, among the strings.
Such instruments are fickle, hothouse things;
you might put one before a *khamsin*, say,
which Brewer salutes as 'a fifty days'

wind in Egypt', and scarcely cop a plink
therefrom. *Pampero, harmattan* and *mistral:*
none can make a troubadour or prink
the tin-eared poetaster's caterwaul.

I, for instance, took my verse box to Peru,
held it in the snapping *puna* gale,
and didn't get so much as doggerel.
Which is why I've traded down to this kazoo,

this rude, barbaric tube whose only note –
a raspberry, Bronx cheer, or lusty troat
chortled by some rutting pinniped
from hell – will sound, if dunderheaded,

at least reliably with every wheeze.
An afflatus stalwart as a caravel
is what I need, one undaunted by the *bise*
of despondency and sloth – no Philomel,

perhaps, but also no fantastic roc
or wild goose gulling me loose from gravity.
Enough of being the zephyrs' shuttlecock,
the passive frisbee of velleities,

a New Age porch chime tinkling in Marin!
Swatted, lofted, jiggered like a kite? Fuck that.
Gimme a strapping muse to insufflate
my lungs with common air, wipe the Hippocrene

bubbles from my mouth – a lifeguard muse of meat
and homefries, not ambrosia, with blood
instead of ichor in her veins. Effete
Parnassians, vamoose: the old amplitude

of paranormal sponsorship has shrunk,
quaint casualty of our vogue to debunk
the very credences that once sustained
these rhapsodies. The wind is now the wind

is just the prolix, tenantless breeze;
a quondam host to pixie orchestras
who played us adventitiously because
we expected them to, its deities

have skedaddled like a rock band breaking up.
Therefore I take my dime-store didgeridoo,
my little pipe of homeliness, my Jew's
harp galumphing out its squawky bop,

my poor kazoo, and, disgrace to Jubal
that I am, honk away without *sirocco*
or buff *nor'easter* in my sails. After all,
as the Latin saw goes, 'When there's no wind, row.'

Hiroshima Without Adjectives
after John Hersey

The panic grass is pushing up
serenity into an air
that has at last regained its pale.

Above the burn, the feverfew,
the goosefoot stepping into view
among the Spanish bayonets.

The epicentre's blank is filled
as sickle senna radiates
its colour outward to the world.

The painter's shadow pressed against
the wall he worked, his ladder too,
his brush about to dip the paint.

There is a man who drove a cart,
the space between his horse and whip,
and all the morning glories growing there.

The Calligraphy Shop

My God, they were all so beautiful,
each parchment trumpeting its cursive praise
of Allah, whose residence in Istanbul

seemed tenuous throughout the vulgar maze
of kitsch and gizmos the Grand Bazaar's become.
Here at last, I thought, He'd find a phrase

or two to please Him – not the vendors' dumb,
kilowatt promotion of their crap,
but silent decibels of script, its un-

or otherworldly characters trapped
in suspended eloquence. As if on ice
a figure-skating rubricant had mapped

his arabesques with slathered blades, the rise
and roller-coaster dip of letters swelled
even past my ignorance; my eyes

alone could estimate, yet not quite melt,
the igneous devotion frozen there.
Did it matter exactly what they spelt?

Arcs, crescents, diamonds punctuating the air
above them: an abstract caravan
of lines carried over crystal-clear

its cargo, the sweet imbroglio of man
and deity snagged (I romanticised)
within those desert skeins. The Koran

fanned out across the walls in bearably sized
divisions of its heat, the surahs all
cooling under glass – some plain, some surprised

alchemically into animals.
There were verses crammed to fit a camel's back,
Kufic exhortations strung along the tails

of tigers like a lash, delicate black
songbirds caged in painstaking minuscule,
and, beside them, brute raptors shellacked

to paper by religion. Such midnight oil
that must have torched, these anonymous
masters of kinetic penmanship, such toil

lavished on the strictly frivolous!
But would their occidental counterparts
have recognised the brotherhood of bliss

between them, the consanguinity of art,
or would the monks behind the Book of Kells
have cried for heathen blood and torn apart

their genius as the stuff of infidels?
As I was pondering this, the store's
proprietor approached, offering his help

in that skewed, courtly English foreigners
can so disarm us with. He laid out
his treasures patiently: which ones were

Turkish, Urdu, what they were about,
the deep antique and the relatively new.
Then, perceiving my attention caught

by a small one high up on the wall, he drew
it closer. Although less extravagant
than others, it fascinated through

sheer obsessiveness, for the inscription went
hypnotically snaking down a gyre.
'Ah yes,' said my host. 'It's Kurdish, meant

to rid a house of demons, djinn, whatever
pesky spirits skulk around. Place a bowl
beneath it, then wait for ghosts to gather.

They will amass, unable to control
their belletristic curiosity.
Once they start to read they'll read the whole,

the spiral pulling them inexorably
toward its centre, from where they drop
into the dish – now disposable, you see.'

And so was I. Powerless to stop
gawking at the paranormal bait
before me, suckered by its agitprop,

toppled by an agile nib, I let
my sceptical guard fall peacefully. Outside,
a muezzin was warbling, from his minaret,

torrid plangencies of prayer and pride
upbraided, his spectral keening parallel
or woven with the printed one I tried,

but failed, to resist, susceptible
as I was that blazing August afternoon
to the Byzantine embellishments of quill

searing the mere vellum. I've come to burn,
since then, with a greedy rage to reproduce
its tyrannies, inflicting in turn

(on fellow ghosts) capture, jail, the gentle noose
of amazement; I've come to hunt its cold,
fatally calibrated charm, its ruse

of hanging there in ambush, growing old.

David Morley

DAVID MORLEY was born in Blackpool in 1964. He read Zoology at Bristol University and gained a Fellowship from the Freshwater Biological Association. He was subsequently awarded a major Eric Gregory Award, and has also received an Arts Council Writers Award, as well as a Hawthornden Fellowship. He was appointed Senior Lecturer at Warwick University in 2002 and is Director of the Warwick Writing Programme.

His books include *Releasing Stone* (Nanholme Press, 1989), *A Belfast Kiss* (Smith Doorstop Books, 1991) and *Scientific Papers* (Carcanet Press, 2002). He is the co-editor of *The New Poetry* (Bloodaxe Books, 1993) and editor of *Jude the Obscure: Thomas Hardy* (Könemann, 2000) and *The Gift: New Writing for the NHS* (Stride Publications, 2002). He is currently working on *Patrin*, the second part of *Scientific Papers*, and *The Cambridge Introduction to Creative Writing*.

Poems in this selection have appeared in *Stand*, the *Independent*, *The Tabla Book of New Poetry*, *The Forward Book of Poetry 2001* and *New Writing 9*, which was edited by John Fowles and A.L. Kennedy, and broadcast on BBC Radio 2 and 3.

12
Clearing a Name

Spindrift across Stalmine, a place you won't know.
Reedbeds, gyp sites; flat Lancashire's Orinoco.

I watch a mistle-thrush on a blown telegraph wire,
leave my car by the dead elm above the river.

The camp is two caravans. The police have just left.
Two blu-tacked Court Orders this wind can't shift

or the rain read. A girl squatting with a carburettor
on her bare knees. Another, older, in a deck-chair

spoons Pot Noodle. Their dad with his pride, no joy,
wrestles over the yawning bonnet of a lorry.

Mam is out, knocking Blackpool's door
with her basket of tack, toddler dressed-down with care

for the rending detail: no shoes. I watch
the father unbend, fumble at the fire, splice a match

from a stray half-wicker, then I come down.
He lets a welcome wait in another time,

twists a roll-up, nods OK to his staring daughters.
Eyes me like fresh scrap fenced from a dealer,

half-sorted, half-known. Yes; he knew our family
'more for what they were' – Hop-girls, Iron-boys –

'but they married out, and there's the end of it.
Your muck's paid no muck of ours a visit'.

A thin smile: 'Except your dad,
he came with the nose of Concorde

on worksheets reeking of grease and swarfega,
bleating "an inch is now a bloody centimetre".

What's up with your schools? I'd say. Him – "This *is* school".
We squinnied blueprints as if they were braille.

Taught ourselves ground-up. A small conversion.
If your muck had stayed in family, if your gran

not gone nosing *gaujo* like they were the end-all.
Now you've had your end, fair do's. Get off pal,

you're not burnt up on fags or dodgy work.'

The ends, we want; the means are half the work:

something in his grip, under my sleeve like veins,
where hands lock together, become the same,

'Arctic on Antarctica' ... *I need background.*
The uncle on my mother's side. 'Pulled from a pond.

The police were out for a man. Any taig or gyp.
Guns broke for a chicken-shoot. They found him face-up

and it fitted. They shot shite in a barrel.'
That B-road where Lancashire discharges its spoil.

Split mattresses. Paint tins. Grim stuff in carriers.
The sign No Dumping No Travellers.

I make my way back to the car, running
the hard keys from hand to hand then, turning,

pocket them. I do not move. It is not smart to show
(that plain car by the woods) how and where you go.

One uncle of mine went swimming. His name is snow,
or thaw, or mud. And you wouldn't know.

13
The Errand

I came to a place where buildings were going up;
biscuits of slate sat wrapped in twine.
Earth moved like sugar, boiling,
against the metal of a dumper.
A machine dropped, dropped its yellow snout
nuzzling at joists it was hammering in.
When I got to my father I would learn
the heat of that impact, how you might
light paper from the surface two hours on.
The air meanwhile would shiver with fire,
a fineless dust, the shouts of impact.

He was with the welders –
a short-term hire – cutting thin plate
to microns. Not visored, he
stood out from that coven
of kneeled and sparking men
like something they were making
or melting to start over.
We went out to sandpiles, pounded stone,
his eyes spindling, his mouth
asking and asking why I was there.

14
Moonlighter

He might be my brother for all he is gyp.
His is not the time for pullovers and combs;
his plum shirt is Blackpool, very Blackpool.
I have watched his van for hours, from Marton Estate

to this traveller site; a mole in mole's clothing.
He will scrabble through the mud of everything:
the nuts and nuggets of marriage, a bolt of a ring,
weights of children, slack pulleys of police.
Burglar by night, a rain-soaked genius
of the jerry-built coastal pre-fab,
he stacks his van with valuables:
a deadman, a handspike, a parbuckle.
Lightning moves its show across the camp.

15
Σ

Our family eats the funeral sandwiches: pink paste and white bread.
My four saucy uncles pinch at their bits of tobacco.
They fall, clawing at fake heart attacks each time I come up to them.

We are in the kitchen of my dead grandmother's maisonette.
Her sisters squawk about compensation, weather, and the Third Eye.
One of my aunts goes spare: 'What's dead is dead.
We're small people. We can't take on the whole bloody NHS.'

The internal pressure burst the capillaries beneath my gran's eye
diagonally, like a whip might, opening her hale cheekbone up.
Sigma is the shape carved on that seventy-year-old face
where the care-worker screwed his fist around her nose to smash it.

16
The Wakes

On the blue, four and two.
On the white, your camera-light.
Blackpool queues, how do you do's.
Blackpool's wealth, the brain's on a shelf.
Knock it back. Bring it up.

Glasgow Wake. Run on the clubs.
The zoo on Sunday, its all-hour pub.
The girls of wire, their tiny men,
the kiss, the rub, the bye bye hymen.
Gold rushed in from the offshore rigs.
The black stuff, cash; the men, the cogs.
Barnsley Wake. The smuts of air,
the skinned-up blow, the Solacare.
Downwind of the weather cock –
Heysham trawlers, Fleetwood Macs,
the Cod War punching at their backs.
The Cod War, the coldest war.
Welsh Wake. The train's a throat
boozing through Preston, cacking through Kirkham,
spuming in the forth of Blackpool North.
The cut-throat cabs, the pugs, the blabs,
the shot up cases, the bastard scabs.
Blackpool queues, the threats, the bruise.
Miner's Wake. Had it good,
then Miners' Strike; Cortonwood.
The Miners' strike, then the English knife.
A policemen's lot: nasty, short.
Blackpool taunts, how do you don'ts.
Blackpool's wealth, the brain's on a shelf.
Irish Wake. Gypsy-speak –
Irish Stew in the name of the bore.
God rushed in to the Belfast yards,
an Irish Card, a prod old guard.
Then the dollar's breath, a year-long death;
a boom, a bust. The shipyard's rust.
Rochdale Wake. Drink till you choke.

Knock it back, dog it up.
Knock her up. Kiss her quick.
Dog her quick. Knock her back.
The North Pier and tackled up.
A haul of fish, the flask. The mug.

Clickety-click, full house, drop-kick.
Blackpool queues, how do you do's.
Blackpool's wealth, the brain's on a shelf.
On the blue, four and two.
On the white, your camera-light.

17
Nature of Memory

It flatters you with its ballet-stretch at the mirror,
a river of trained movements, its yawn and shiver –
waiting for you to call it into the world.
But above all, it flatters you.

Your brain is a sea. A memory
buoys, a private prodigality:
a red, laden ship in a limestone harbour,
dredgers drag its beaten shore.

Difficult, a memory is clearly sorrow.
It lies to you like your cornered boy
holding out his colourful plan
for an imaginary land built by him and for him.

18
Friendly and Equitable Insurance

I've been out in the woods and brought something home.
A creature, no, nor lichen sleeved from a branch.
I've been digging, not to lay a ghost
or to find a father, but to uncover the taproot
of that famous tree from the book of memory.
I post myself a report on its territory:
a nervous system of root, the brain of leaf,
perennial synapses of forgettings and rememberings.
And when I receive it I will not believe in it;
bin it with my father and all the creatures,
dead or imagined, not worth the risk,
a risk that could make me hate myself.

The next morning I will not go to the woods.
I'll read about my death by easy payments.
For if my eyelash offends I pluck it.
If the city grows too hot I leave it,
hitting the countryside with its big-hearted hedges,
vistas and many sites of historical interest.
In everything I do, I offend something.
The taproot oozes oil, spreads across my memory,
blacks and confuses it. I must do as I please
with this sunlit morning: the light is accurate
and I stand square as though I owned it.
As though I deserved it no more.

Togara Muzanenhamo

Togara Muzanenhamo was born in Lusaka, Zambia (to Zimbabwean parents) in 1975. He was brought up in Zimbabwe then went on to study Business Administration in The Hague and Paris. After his studies he became a journalist for a state-owned paper in Harare, then was employed by a film script development institution.

Togara's poems have appeared in various magazines and journals in England, France, South Africa and Zimbabwe. In 2001 he was a recipient of a writer's bursary granted by the North West Arts Board.

Hawker (Johannesburg)

Drawing up to a stop-street,
The hawkers approached –
Drawing themselves thinner
By pulling in their elbows
And holding goods over their groins.

Squeezing between cars,
One holds polystyrene model gliders,
Another licence stickers,
One, below the red stop-sign,
Holds a poetry book

With my name beneath the title.
He looks like me.
He has my smile tucked within
His left hand shirt pocket.

Winter

We retrieve seasonal blankets from the linen closet,
Wear heavy socks that disguise our crippled feet,
Hiding frost marks of where we tread at night.

Sesame buns and bowls of onion soup
Sit on the kitchen table in impatient light
That rushes off, falling over the slope of the horizon –
Missing all trees, anthills and waking noctivagants.

8.10pm, the radio shut off. We stare at the dead
Bar heater on the cold hearth of the fire place
– As the gas lamp's flame hums (its blue sternum stiff –
And bright white head dispersing);

Mother cuts the cold with the flick of a page,
The leather cover of her Bible frozen in the lap of her
Knotted rug. She whispers Amen with another slice;
Father's ghost sniffs behind the glass –

Revealed between the curtains' gap.

Summer

Entangled in the thyme bush lay an adder's slough,
Left there to keep us wary as we plucked the needle leaves.
From the scullery window, overlooking borage and fennel,
Was the view of the pondweed's tall thin stipes.

We'd go there – surrounded by dragonflies and anopheles;
Reap bulrushes' velvet heads, place them in creels of plaited reeds –
Then sit beneath the willow peeling green stalks of papyri,
Drying their pith, in the sun, to stick-pens that snapped with ease.

Within the shallow pool a great lizard lay belly up –
Flies sailed upon the white bloated bulge, and the buoyant under tail
Formed a quay for more flies to land.
We'd smell the stagnant water air, pinch our noses tight,

Hold our breaths then breathe the air again.
Nothing could be wrong, not even the swale's putrid smell
Kept us from doing it all again, the next day with our return;
Reaping bulrushes' heads, barefoot, in the cool mud.

Revisiting Hotel Rooms

At night, always the curtains drawn over a wide view of a city without a moon. The beds – always a pale colour. The carpets – a sturdy scrub of deep earth tones, quick foot-steps vacuumed.

No mints beneath the pillows anymore – just dreams cozened by compliment cards, soft music, dimmer-lamps, lifeless reproductions of Gauguin, Klimt, or watercolour landscapes frozen beneath a floe of framed glass.

Next door is always a couple. They order room service, drink white wine or champagne, fill the passageways with trays of unfinished meals and half empty glasses. They fuck loud – thud against the wall, watch late-night television, sing in the shower; you know them at reception – she holds his arm and whispers in his ear.

When morning comes the light takes time to settle. Keys rattle in the narrow passageways, doors slyly open, trays and sheets are loaded on squeaking trolleys.

You draw the curtains and somehow the windows were never that small, that loud last night; and the streets below, adorned with tiger stripe sun and shadow, are uncomfortably foreign. Unsealing the window all time escapes rashly; and yet I let my sight fall to the ground below – my eyes comb through the intrusion of tall buildings upon the sky.

Morning

They dehorned the bulls not far from the house,
By the cattle dip – that was always upwind.
The smell of burning nails would enter the windows,
On early mornings between six and eight.

Father was there – leaning attentively over
Wooden beams painted with *carnabellum*.
At breakfast he came into the kitchen
Smelling of cattle dung, treated wood, fresh sweat.
He had a full breakfast: bread, tomatoes,
Coffee, and fried eggs.

As we realigned the chains on our bicycles
He casually walked out of the yard,
Back to the paddocks from which the
Smell of smouldering horns came.

We rode down to where he stood,
Leaning over the beams of treated wood;
'Father,' we said, 'doesn't that hurt?'
and the labourers laughed –

Calling us *varungu*,
And we'd hide behind father's sturdy frame
With our cheeks pressed tight on the khaki pockets
That sloped over his buttocks.

He would say 'No', calmly –
And the air filled with the smell of burned hair
Reminding us of grandmother's iron comb
Heating on the burning stove.

The cattle jerked as each one's neck
Was held in the iron girdle,
Their feet stomped, heaving dust to where we stood.

We looked at their eyes, bovine holes of fear;
With our cheeks pressed tight on the khaki trousers
That sloped over father's buttocks.

Captain of the Lighthouse

The late hour trickles to morning. The cattle low profusely by the anthill where brother and I climb and call Land's End. We are watchmen overlooking a sea of hazel-acacia-green, over torrents of dust whipping about in whirlwinds and dirt tracks that reach us as firths.

We man our lighthouse – cattle as ships. We throw stones as warning lights whenever they come too close to our jagged shore. The anthill, the orris-earth lighthouse, from where we hurl stones like light in every direction.

Tafara stands on its summit speaking in *sea-talk*, Aye-aye me lad – a ship's a-coming! And hurls a rock at the dumb cow sailing in. Her beefy hulk stupidly jolts and turns. Aye, Captain, another ship saved! I cry and furl my fingers into an air-long telescope – searching for more vessels in the day-night.

Now they low on the anthill, stranded in the dark. Their sonorous cries haunt through the night. Aye, methinks, me miss my brother, Captain of the lighthouse, set sail from land's end into the deepest seventh sea.

Coat

Father hangs in the open closet,
A body with no hands or legs.
His shoes – in the shadow beneath;
Side by side, shoelaces tied –
Feet could still be in them.

It hangs like a carcass in a cold-room.
A black piece of meat – headless.
Hung by a hook curling over the rail –
Shoulders drooping, a numbered
White tag pinned to the lapel.

I shan't sleep tonight – staring there,
Staring into that vault where things are hung;
The last thing of him, the one thing I will never
Dare to wear.

The breast pocket could be a heart. Empty, still.

(13.iii.b – from October)

One by one Father would take us into his arms, cradle us for
a moment – rocking us; then from his god-like strength we
were flung like memories into the unsure as we soared up, fell
and splashed into the pool.

There was a safety and imagined danger in this game; he stood
at the edge of the pool like a machine manufacturing joy as we
ran into his arms like components into an assembly line, to be
hurled into absolute completion, again.

10.i (from October)

Deer in the park, seconds from The Hague's Central Station.
Dierentuin was one of the first Dutch words I learnt. The
creatures looked so fragile and misplaced behind the wrought-
iron fence, yet also strangely unperturbed as a tram reeled by
– startling my father and I as we crossed the rails.

We passed a funfair; tents with bright festive lights, a miniature
Catherine-wheel burning out with slowing sparks – twirling
to extinction, defunct and pitiful in that ending carnival.

On we walked in search of our hotel, our bags clanging and
scrapping at our heels, constantly searching the foreign road for
a taxi. A man we had asked directions said the hotel was within
walking distance, *'Just up the road, around the corner – over the
bridge and then a left,'* he said.

But up the road was confusion, where time stalled and drew
in our fatigued bodies as we walked searching for either taxi or
bridge.

5.iii (windmills – from October)

For hours we'd station ourselves, on our bellies, in front of
three scaled-down replicas of windmills – blowing into them
on the sand-coloured carpet, watching their metal sails rotate,
hypnotised by their silver spin.

We were caricatured clouds, the ones in cartoons: full cheeks
blowing westward, eastward, northward and south – watching
their vanes perform simple magic from an exhale.

We competed to see who could turn the blades fastest – then shouted into the rotation to hear our voices cut, cut, cut ... to fragments of loaded air – our words sliced to coded messages, nearly secrets.

And in our chants of nonsense I'd *sing* the world away – wish to be complete; but the blades kept spinning then slowed down to an unyielding pace, coming to halt like a forgotten promise.

10.iv (from October)

The train slurred to a stop from Paris. The transition of language was blurred, noted by the occasional poster or advertisement in Flemish. The information board was twice the size for reasons of compromise: next stop was *Antwerp*, *Antwerpen*, and *Anvers*.

From there on, along the track, staring out into flat farmyards and clustered villages, one wondered where the change of language and idiom began, changed tongues or hands:

Perhaps beneath the tree swiftly passing by, as we rode on, or over a boundary fence in a sparse wheat-field in no-man's-land.

I read a book and drank a glass of red wine in the transforming restaurant, from bar to diners car, as day changed over to night.

A woman I had spoken to, previously in French, in the passenger carriage, sat down next to me after ordering a meal and said, 'Wij zijn bijna, Antwerpen is dichtbij.' And I replied, as though nothing had changed, 'Ja, ik heb meer huisen opgemerkt.'

11 (wedding picture – from October)

On the mantelpiece, a verdite frame: a faded sepia photograph depicts a young couple thronged by a motionless crowd. The crowd is singing, dancing beneath the eaves of a hut where dust has risen from bare feet, the cloud suspended in time forever.

She holds indistinct flowers, the bride, dressed in white; he is all bravado – standing straight and sturdy like a tree trunk severed just below its first branch. The best man, much shorter than the groom, looks to the ground as though he consults my father's shadow, but in actuality is only whispering a joke.

And much the same as then – he looks down now, though no joke, into a grave – a throng of dancers, singing and grieving as my father's coffin is lowered into the shadowed hole and my mother throws a lily to the descending casket, and both seem to fall for ever.

Excursions

All four windows open, on an empty road. Saturday afternoon – returning from a day-trip in the Eastern Highlands, the radio at top volume, the car gunning at well over a hundred miles an hour – my nephew and niece loving it all, strapped down in the back seat of the car.

School days, when I was their age on excursions, we'd chant for the bus driver to put his foot down; 'Go driver! Go! – Go! Driver Go!' each refrain gaining volume, our chants growing wilder and wilder till the bus was a vessel of screaming air.

The boys at the back stuck their heads out the windows and ate *speed*, had their mouths drawn dry as they screamed through the thrill. The *less fortunate* ones, in front or in the aisles, either thumped their fists into the upholstered seats or drummed their feet on the iron floor as the driver tested the bus's limits – inebriated by the chants of frenzied children hailing him as god;
'Go driver! Go!
Go driver! Go!'

I turned off the highway, the electronic windows sliding upward, cutting out the dust along the dirt track leading to the homestead; air conditioning on, the German car rolling into the garage as safe as warm honey twirling into a jam jar.

Ian Pindar

IAN PINDAR was born in London in 1970 and was educated at Lady Margaret Hall, Oxford, where he took a First in English Language and Literature. He began reviewing for the *Times Literary Supplement* in 1992. He has been an editor at various publishing houses, including Weidenfeld & Nicolson and The Harvill Press, but is now freelance. His translation (with Paul Sutton) of Félix Guattari's *The Three Ecologies* appeared in 2000. He is writing a biography of James Joyce and lives in Brixton, London.

Parasite

They breed on the branches of trees,
Colonise the land, seek safety in numbers
And keep moist by drinking sugary soft drinks.

Vulnerable to the vagaries of the global economy,
They come upon white shores, ignorant of the inhabitants,
Utter brief words, build bridges and sing of ages past.

Their children are small and brown well into adulthood,
When they are bought and sold, dropped from great heights
Into enemy territory to become

Bleached bones and souvenirs, perhaps
A television documentary, if they are lucky.
The unlucky are soon forgotten.

After a decade of treading water
He recalls his optimistic youth,
Broods on abandoned loves, lost friends, dead-end jobs . . .

A line of boulders at the front door cannot be shifted.
He must find a new home, dashes out onto the plains,
Follows predators and slams doors.

At midnight he plays the Blues.
He is continually searching for her on long journeys.
She haunts him everywhere and communicates by shrill,
                              high-pitched shrieks.

Call to Arms

Generalissimo, your pants are too tight.
Führer, you have unsightly body hair.

You wrote years before
Of mass executions and waging war.

When you came to power in your black coat
It was in the nature of a side-show.

The professional criminals, the younger generation,
Weren't so talented as you made out.

Instruments of tyranny reappear,
Their bodies exhumed, all in uniform, ready to fight.

The final link in the chain: a camp
For naughty boys. The whole party was taken prisoner.

Forceps in hand, a gallery of rogues
Abandoned the professional standards of their calling.

It makes no difference to me if your people starve.
Having escaped the slaughter and received no wound,

I took advantage of a cloud of smoke
To hide behind the altar.

Casanova

He is unique, like everyone else.
There is no second chance, no afterlife.
All he wants is to be a real Casanova,
Give his partner complete satisfaction,
Clear his existing credit,
Amaze his friends with his feats of memory,
Save money on a lawnmower.

He can go neither forwards nor backwards.
They mock his accent, astonish him with their predictions.
He tries to kill his adopted son.
The walls of the room fall away to reveal
A cement horizon. He waits for his connection.

Work

Permanently angry, hyper-rational to the point of delirium,
They work from an unventilated factory in blistering heat,
Drink rain water, live in unsanitary overcrowded barracks.

They believe in nothing at all,
Auto-analysis, a chemistry of feelings.
At night he sniffs the panties she gave him at the station,
And ejaculates over his belly. They fight to lick him clean,
Hungry for protein.

The book is progressing, mixing,
Dismantling, reassembling,
In accordance with cosmic forces
(Which he calls 'oscillation').
It comes as no surprise
It is impossible to summarise.

Nobody is in charge, for the time being.

Greek

Left alone, you grow from the experience
A black beard.

A black beard and a head teeming with ideas,
Some of them really weird

But hardly unique;
Entertained long ago by a Greek.

Even the beard.

Shampoo

A New Year, new violence in the region.
Countries open and close their borders
In time for their favourite soap operas.

The activities of imagined people are as real
As their own lives. But politics
Has no appeal.

A man can go a long way
With hair so dandruff free and attractive
It's irresistible.

But if he were to go my way
He would find
A talent for halfway realised projects,

A troubled mind, a fluid state of ignorance,
A life of solitude and shocks,
A body wrapped in a shroud.

That is why I am as controversial as I am famous.
Burning rags are shoved through my letterbox
And I play to a sell-out crowd.

Kissing

On our last day,
When I kissed you so passionately,
You had every right
To bite off my tongue and spit it out.

Instead you cried. I cried two
Days later, listening to a Jew
On the radio describe
How he survived Auschwitz
By the skin of his teeth.

The skin.
The teeth.

Red Sunglasses

Before you poisoned the water
We drank to the health
Of your wayward daughter:
'May she find love, wealth
And happiness,' we said.
Now she is dead.

They came upon her in a clearing
Of scorched grass and litter.
Her naked body beaten all over
And her head missing.

I wish you had called her earlier,
Had told her you loved her
Like a dad should. Instead
You lectured to a bored crowd
On the dangers of walking on water,
With subtitles for the hard of hearing.
I wish you had called her earlier
And told her you loved her.

Faschismus

They will be smiling like they did of old,
Keeping tradition in the blood
And blood in the soil.

Men of action, irrational,
Suspicious of intellect: all dissent
Is betrayal and betrayal death.

Fear difference: the enemy
Within. If you are weak
You will die, as Nature intended.

And the people perish,
Reeling, staggering towards
A ring of light on the horizon.

Eveline

Far from the details of his daily life
He accosts strangers in search of relief,
Compares each conquest to his wife.

But she was never so familiar,
Nor so apparent in her moods. Her
Pleasures brief and irregular.

Now she is waiting in the family home
Darning a sock or dusting a beam.
Walking, he whispers her name.

Sue Roe

SUE ROE was born in Leicester in 1956, and was educated at the universities of Kent and Sussex. Her most recent book is *Gwen John: A Life* (Chatto & Windus and Farrar, Straus & Giroux, 2001; Vintage, 2002). She is a freelance writer and editor whose previous books include a novel, *Estella, Her Expectations* (Harvester, 1982; 1983); a critical study, *Writing and Gender: Virginia Woolf's Writing Practice* (Harvester, 1990) and a selection of poems, *The Spitfire Factory* (Dale House Press, 1998). She is editor of Virginia Woolf's *Jacob's Room* (Penguin Modern Classics, 1992) and co-editor of *The Cambridge Companion to Virginia Woolf* (2000).

Of the poems in this selection, 'The Spitfire Factory' first appeared in Sue Roe's *The Spitfire Factory*. 'Contained' first appeared in *The Charleston Magazine*, Autumn/Winter, 1999. 'On Seeing St Teresa's Arm in Alba' was runner-up in the Yorkshire Poetry Competition, 1997.

The Spitfire Factory

I don't know what world this is but I know it
the factory windows are smashed in beautiful crystals
square by devastated square
and the size of it is like owning the sea
when you press two buttons, put a crazed-shaped key
in a small lock and push the heavy metal
you open an enormous door
on a world of interiors that echo, echo, echo

every door is tall, every room
a citadel, a disused church, the empty ammunitions factory
where they used to make wings, the wings of spitfires, the wings
of fighters, of enemy action, the kinds of wings
that have left this place unused and billowing out
aching to be inhabited by one or two
to make up for the exit of thousands, the exit of millions
all using their hands in synchronicity
in feathery movements day after day, night after night
shift after shift, making wings.

I don't know what world this is but I know it
as after decades of being away, the immaculate floors
pitted with sore soles, the aching ankle bones
of people standing up, clicking wings for hours on benches.
Now there are drawings on the walls
great canvases showing space endlessly receding,
and a child's drawings, made with bright collages
of tickets and stickers, coloured thoroughly over.
When I wander out into the passages
the world echoes floor to ceiling with the emptiness
full from side to side, end to end, of hands working
when I turn the tap on blackened hands
cover a small ball of soap with charcoal, cover it
over and over under the coursing water
I find myself looking into an empty corner

just an empty corner, stained with a watermark
and that's what I'm seeing everywhere, all over
this vascular place, its scarred, pitted walls
reverberating with the sound of going back strongly
to a place I could shout about in this time, shout
sing, run, remember, throw stones
and this time they'd spin across the top
of the water, move through on skates
and this time I wouldn't fall over,
arrive for curtain-up and it would be my cue
take the applause, go back down to my dressing room ...

I don't know how to see anything in space.
I have moved into a factory-sized place, for millions
of wings, and all I'm bringing
is a sheet of sugar paper, sticks of charcoal
a putty rubber, an arrangement of forms,
knowing I could dance this floor.
The light changes as we're standing here
in two small hours like stones new tones
roll around my shells, moving around in pools
on the floor I make. I don't know how to record
this, or any of it. But I know I know
that something in these walls is ours, something
that fell out once, from the leaves of a book, the wings
of women, all their fathers and forefathers,
is held in places like this, where they made spitfires.

Already I am planning my summer wardrobe
already I am planning my summer child
already it doesn't matter so much about that winter
that lasted so many years, or about the women
who fled for their lives, left us without a story.
Something about the walls does this, something
about something somebody left behind without saying
just how far out we'd have to go to retrieve it
how much we'd have to say before we could say it
how some places are open, some are closed
how many times you have to be trapped in enclosed
closets before it's safe to open the door
look into a place like this and to hell with spitfires.

When the sun moves round the walls I can see wings
and it doesn't matter so much now about factories
because now they're finally closed for business they're open
to summer about to pick itself obviously out
in yellow and purple crocuses like shells
the green, bright eyes of a child, his feathered drawing
with feathers of all colours, rivulets of sand
and the child turning it, turning it to see which way
it has to be to show the mother bird
which you'll certainly see, if he can just see which way up it is
and canvases hung for their colours
work to be done for no reason
except to let us trespass between the leaves
to detect the whisper of voices we thought had died
to play for our lives, now, in the spitfire factory.

Rain

Like rain that has stopped, and afterwards
walking to the car and finding it
still there, and the surprising hair
everywhere that summer, on wrists
tents, latex curved torsos hanging
from the wall with the naked dancer
with a broken spine,
etched in sharp pencil,
lightly

getting up after getting wet
shaking ourselves like red umbrellas
telling ourselves jokes we told ourselves
were neither very funny nor particularly clever
laughing like drains
finding ourselves again
at the car door, sliced between us
a staggering gash of metal
still slightly wet after the downpour
not ready yet for the dew

I couldn't believe you
could stand like a blasted tree, so much of you
sheered off, the pink, the supple wood
open to the night, held together
with a few brown clothes, like sparse bark
or a letter no one should really be reading
pinned like a butterfly, preceded by
its own envelope, its own postmark.

Here is another day
with rain again, but rain
like a shut bathroom door, sheeting down
solid as strings, loud
as a soloist heard up close.
Nothing much changes
except when the rain is red
the car door wriggles on its pin
before midnight, and they say lightning
never ever strikes in the same place twice,
never strikes twice in a place like this.

Tapapau

I was a stiff girl
in a striped dress
holding a mandolin

you were a sleeping lion
waiting for the turn of the year
holding your secrets in

I talked to you many times
but you always said a lion
would never say anything

the year cracked down
lay like a felled tree
I heard you whisper to me

and the sound of the mandolin
came softly on animal strings
the scent of a lion breathing

you said *don't speak, don't sing,*
don't move, don't do anything
the spirits will do everything

her dress is hot and loud
can't you hear it singing?
the stars are whispering.

On Seeing Saint Teresa's Arm in Alba

This memory, of riding through the street
on a bus from school, the top deck of the bus
and seeing, propped on a sill, two perfect feet

seems to have nothing to do with the scrap of meat
rolled between silver, causing genuflections, fuss,
people pushing forward, pulling back, meek

giving of coins into hands, this overwhelming, sweet
shrivelled carrot seems to be soft but surely must
be hard as an old hassock, must surely reek

of camphor, white spirit, turps, neat
alcohol. Where are the veins? trussed
up quite tightly, packed in like a discreet

undergarment, like coins in a pouch, a sick bag in a seat
it bends like a baby's spine, looks tough and fusty
as an antimacassar, rank as a roll of peat.

I remember the plaque on the gate onto the street
displaying the dancer's credentials in brass and rust.
Now I can see her dancing: Saint Teresa
dancing through Alba, whirling along the street.

Magi

I have tucked a shining angel
into the trunk of the fir tree
scarlet, spruce, gold
be-ribboned, little Babushka

her celestial sisters
are bringing frankincense
and myrrh, waiting in the branches
for the first, just-audible stir

of millions of slumbering children
it is theirs, this story of snow,
singing, the star, the cold coming
to birth: it is theirs, it is theirs.

Contained

they kept their own distance and their own counsel
the green-fingered house, angular, watery tank
where she folded her long legs under the desk
her grasshopper mind picking its way like blades
turning up Gibbon, Meredith, the Greeks
across waves and swathes of time, all hair and bones

and the soft, fine lavender mist
of a house with its low, deep hearth
ringing out with its pastel tones, its silent notes
Mrs Grant doing her needlework
the economic consequences weighed and felt
against laughter in the garden, the pale grey glow

the Downs kept them separate and together
their chalky breasts measuring the breadth
of differences dropped beneath
the burning glass of the land:
the voices of children, the undertow
of birds still singing in the gloaming

the drag of sitting to the task while the talk
began rising, its green surface flickering
and flaming, fanning out into the hardness
of phrases, tight-knit as brushes,
wide as a ring, a hoop
dark as the stamping of a beast

the silences of the beach
(were they turning their backs on flesh
wanting to rise, themselves, to a fine, white point?)
the exceptional twist in the snail
borrowed from a dark, damp stain:
Da Vinci's mark on the wall

what are we stealing, rising and falling here
ourselves, wandering stealthily
dazed among the delphiniums
peering into the study in the garden
wanting to touch the table of pastel circles
imagining the wet, green reeds

a light or a dark thing, soft or angular
– hard in the coal scuttle, wisping up thin from a cheroot
our feet on the red rugs, finger-marks on the walls –
painted in pigmented, many-plaited words
the hush of things unsaid, the secrets of houses
the way they rise up green, beat grey against stone

Ferns, from the Stairwell

how I cried out when I saw them sticking up like that
piercing the cellophane, opaque jagged pincers
coming up the stairs in your arms like guns
irises tucked in secretly like tongues

how high they were, arching up in pussy willows
soft as a baby's arms, reminding me of childhood
hard and high as lecterns, their stems thick as childhood
unbending as day, grey as the cold, old Infants

it is not your fault that you came at the blackest hour
I had no idea, when I saw ferns coming up the stairs in your arms
how angry as a mad, black ox I was, how angry as a gun,
how hard my tongue would be when it lashed out words

I had no idea, when I saw the roof of your black hair
how like a bayonet I would be, how like an unshed tear

The Daughters of Truth

His fantasy is the daughter of truth
                    Apollinaire on Bonnard

The daughters of truth are dying
In a blaze of orange light
Look at Marthe's green mules, how
They might have strutted in those!

They are sitting up straight at the table
Ghosts of shade at the window playing
Hide and seek in the red cupboard
Camouflaged with the jam

The daughters of truth are drowning
In a bath that made their mother's flesh
Atrophy for the painter
Making his marks

The surface glitters
Folded round screens and sliding frames,
wrapped in a clutter of colour,
Taking in a little tidy dog

What shall we say to the daughters of truth
Who gave up their chance to play for the art
Of making the beautiful fruit,
Their faces lit in ellipses of flaming orange

The daughters of truth are silent,
Their voices soak in jars by the door.
         See, they depart,
         See, they return.

Antony Rowland

ANTONY ROWLAND was born in Bradford in 1970. He was educated at the University of Hull and the University of Leeds. He now teaches English Literature and Creative Writing at the University of Salford. He has had poems published in the following journals and magazines: *Critical Quarterly*, *Leviathan Quarterly*, *Staple*, *Poetry and Audience*, *Psychopoetica* and *Yorkshire Journal*. He received an Eric Gregory Award for his poetry in 2000, and a Northwest Learning Award in 2001. Antony has also published a critical volume, entitled *Tony Harrison and the Holocaust* (Liverpool University Press, 2001). He is currently working on his first poetry collection, and on critical books on Carol Ann Duffy and Holocaust poetry respectively.

'Cech Speaks' first appeared in *Poetry and Audience*; 'Golem' in *Staple*; and 'Mistle from 1900' in *Critical Quarterly*. All of the poems apart from 'Pomfret' were included in the manuscript which won the Eric Gregory Award.

Cech Speaks

I name a hill a mountain. Ríp.
I consult my map. It is blank (apart from Ríp)
so I name a stream after my elbow
and the land after myself.
Lech forks north and founds Poland.
He cannot face three-word I-Spy,
or years of Smâžény syr.

Wenceslas, neither king nor good,
crisps a snowball with the tongues
of St Vitas's gargoyles in his sights.
Terezín bleeds afresh 'ARBEIT MACHT FREI'.
Tanks pock the National Museum,
shells smack a raspberry surface
that hides marble, not the parliament.

Stâre Mésto could be St Michael's Mount,
were it not for the villa's facade,
which crumbles behind state perfection
to a rot of sump and public toilets.
Guards slurp in a hut lapped by the Vltava,
waiting with sandwiches for Vaclav Haval.
Ice cream cones flash in Wenceslas Square.

Golem

We come from beyond the Slovak pail
to find snails on nippy streets
the Sunday rain washed the Vltava plain.
A cat roils a washing line with drops
watching us pale from the CSA plane.
A dog nips at our shadows, barking for sun
and the balmy simplicity of Czech afternoons
but it is as warm as when Rabbi Löw glued
his golem together from Vltava turf.

With you in a pivnice, chilled by wine
bubbling with the graves of Vyšehrad
engraved in your camera, a tomb
for the embarrassment of tourists.
You long for foxes in the Southern Cemetery,
not the thin, spooky statues heavening here.
Your arm gooses when I brush it
by a mausoleum, your lilac smile
like light frosted on the white walls.

We sit like fish as a street boy slips
a backpacker's bag from a Coke cafe.
The velvet revolution is a trail
of brown amok in our red and white cups.
As we eat ice cream in Wenceslas Square
(neither square, nor good),
Russian bears pause in the National Museum,
frozen in a language I can barely understand.
Take my hand. Feel the sundae heat.

Vienna

The average Austrian is happy with some soup followed by
Palatschinken (sweet pancakes), *Topfenstrudel* (special cheese-
cake) or *Apfelstrudel;* a huge variety of sweet or savoury *Knödel*
(dumplings); pasta with eggs or sweet pasta with nuts or poppy
seeds. However, tourists are offered *Schnitzel* ...

                                                    Fatima Martin, Surrey

A shrine for Eagles. Fascism.
Coffee with frothy bite and shots
and cake where no one dares eat it
save the unforeigned, unafraid of fat,
the blood of Blutwurst, the sour of Kraut,
and Hitler's glaze down Schottenring, a lance
clocked in the Schatzkammer that launched his creed.

Clouds glipped with sun pass the Oper, red.
No one reads print squinted in Resistance museums,
paragons to Communist virtue, Austria a victim,
whereas the KunstHaus gluts with camera flash
and lamps too expensive to own. Alone,
Hundertwasser's paint splashes clash with clear Dunkelbier
and soot that felts the fuzz of St Stephen's roof.

Vienna is a cathedral
stained with windows of indelible history,
Babel above, as tourists sift the isles sacked
by the fossilised offal of catacombs below.
Waiting in Albertinaplatz, hosted by cherubs,
an iron Jew rests by empty monuments.
He is still, scrubbing.

Damrak

White rabbits greet the eve of September
on Rokin, a street which leaves a hole
in Amsterdam. Our temporary home
is shabby as the fubs in The Flying Dutchman;
our carpets are the texture of droog brood.
In our rucksack, a nibble of cracker packets.
Autumn comes with a creeping hush.

This city is a giddy kipper.
This bridge is a lekker in an icing of stream.
Crepuscular roads of water are
dreamed by seekers of skunk;
fingers twitch in bottomless pockets.
Dante's waterways concentricised Hell;
the lidless eyes of tourists pass.

Your face as grey as an absent tulip,
we grace Damrak, stationed by a rusp of canals.
A heron freezes the obelisk of a barge.
Pigeons boozle loose air in Singel.
ECUs rise like metaphysical bees
from these thin roofs atop with hooks.
The single sun is a Gogh, ocherous.

The waiters are as elusive as ciscos
in the brown bar, The Three Quarks, marking
the discos of Dam Square. Round the Vondelpark:
flesh, sand and guitars, all bad.
The fat porks glisten in the Indian heat.
In the Twin Pigs, banana bunches peek
like yellow spiders over the bowls.

We have forgotten your mother for a night
but the hotel is still the edge of a nightmare.
Our nostrils pickle with Damrak's sough
as, reflecting neon, mushrooms and windows,
our owner gnomes on Warmoesstraat
with Sunday smiles and hosepipes.
An aubade of dealers flushes the cobbles.

Mistle from 1900

On Woodhouse Ridge, the hills are still
quilted with flowing stone. Below,
William Rowland rivets shoes for life.
Astronauts are ghosts
clumping his mind where money burns
and motorways din to its cusp.

It is 1896.
A keen frost sips at the veins.
He sits on a roof of a school,
pooling his lenses for Jupiter's moons.
Sanded all winter, they are darkly poised.

There is the hand of a dead man on my bookshelf:
his letters shiver on a yellow sheet.
I am thumbing his son's indentures.
He cleaves me with a century,
years of stars, light years younger.

My grandad is a twinkle.
His love was plants, not planets.
I see him bellamy through rubber leaves
preening the edges for the pith of thrips.

In the year of the thrush,
William's prize glass hairlines.
His head whites overnight
but he remains aloft,
only days away from the grave,
imbibing cobblers to astral clusters.

Pomfret

(i.m. Thomas Rowland, 1915–2001)

During the ides of pyres of feet and mouths,
your joints are cooling in the living room.
You leave in your last ambulance and then
the calm in the departed house is colossal;
I wait on your doorstep, and meet a door.

The wake candles your home with relatives:
an aunt is on the fritz with an affidavit
for a teapot which hints at your wrists;
some saw you as a gimmer with a fat sandwich,
evenings measured with tea and fig biscuits
as your thews drew closer to hospital beds.

I see your coffin of my mind and cross
memories part up Barkerend Road:
the shock of your box amongst traffic.

Those little cakes of Pontefract not fish
are unnibbled beside the curtailed shopping list;
sweet meat accompanies the easing of your pulse.

Our last conversation was of dripping:
your laughter and cooking an antidote
to an empty home and calendar,
save 'library', 'library', and 'hair'.

G.I. Joe Flips

'We are trying to make a statement about the way
toys can encourage negative behaviour in children.'
(Barbie Liberation Organisation spokesperson)

I roast Ken by the toaster,
win Barbie and barbecue her.
I don't like cliff-hangers
so I bivouac in the sink
and lick a pink socket.

Then they ambush me.
My genitalia are erased.
I am strung up
and left to rot on a doorknob.
My head is scalded

until the stubble bleeds.
My eagle-eyes are wiggled
until I see my ghost.
My Y-fronts are branded
into folds of skin.

Then they swap my box with hers.
No more vengeance or eating lead,
just, 'Let's plan a dream wedding!'
'Will we have enough clothes?'
and 'Shopping is such fun!'

Chestnut Avenue

The morning toothbrush comes too soon
after the evening moved from caribou to carobs,
and the way your chutney looks like chyme.
Our talk cut short by the kettle's skittling,

I wrinkled in its surface, my cheeks perfected back,
face slack with tea-steam and tears for Sunday,
the glare of kisses in forecourts, a shame
the lines are unhindered with leaves or snow.

Back home, my yukka laps the draught.
Chestnuts butt the flue with feathered fruit.
Galey with rain, sycamores lisp.
The leaves brush with your fingertips.

James Sutherland-Smith

JAMES SUTHERLAND-SMITH was born in Aberdeen in 1948 and was educated at Leeds University. He currently lives in Slovakia, where he is a British Council lecturer. He set up the first Creative Writing Course in English in Central Europe, using writers from Britain and Ireland. His books include *A Poetry Quintet* (Gollancz, 1976) *At the Skin Resort* (Arc, 1999) and *Selected Poems in Slovak* translated by Ján Gavura (Tich voda, 2002) and his poems have been included in a number of anthologies and magazines, including *Thumbscrew* and *Rialto*.

Of the poems in this selection, 'A Roasting Piglet' has been published in *Poetry Wales;* 'Rainoo Repeats Her English in Bombay' was awarded a Special Mention at the *TLS* Poetry Competition (1988) and a Poetry Award by the San Jose Studies (1991). 'South District Prague' won second prize in the Bridport Competition (1998) and has been published in the *Cumberland Poetry Review;* 'Incident in Guatemala' has been published in Ambit; 'At Huwailah Beach' won a San Jose Studies Poetry Award (1991). 'A Snail in Istanbul' was awarded a Special Mention in the *TLS* Poetry Competition (1988) and has been published in *Poetry* (Chicago). 'In the Country of Birds' won first prize in the Robert Penn Warren Poetry competition (2001). 'The Fossil' won third prize in the *TLS* Poetry Competition (1986); 'The Drowned Boy' won fifth prize in the National Poetry Competition (1983) and 'Magnolia' has been published in *The Six Seasons Magazine* (Bangladesh).

A Roasting Piglet

I gave a lift to a man.
He was slightly the worse for drink
And the mapwork on his face
Showed that he and alcohol were always close.

I gave a lift to a man.
The day was chilly and here
There's little threat from a stranger
Except becoming very drunk.

I drove him to his cabin in the woods.
He invited me for coffee
And pressed a triple vodka on me
Which had to be gulped down in one.

We and his friends watched a piglet
Turning slowly on a metal spit
Driven by a motor with a husky purr
Like a queen cat giving birth.

Elsewhere a government had changed.
Elsewhere NATO prepared to bomb the Serbs.
My man basted and sprinkled herbs
As fat dripped and charcoal spluttered.

The pig's jaws gaped round one end of the spit.
The other end came out through a thigh.
Its legs and trotters were folded back.
It could have knelt for the butcher's knife.

We laughed when my man took a cloth
And wiped bubbles from its fizzing snout.
Its ears crisped, the slash across its throat
Cooked from red to gold. I took my leave.

Elsewhere I had paths to sweep,
Mushrooms to pick beside roaring water.
Elsewhere I had other fish to fry,
A piglet of my own to slaughter.

Rainoo Repeats her English in Bombay

Rainoo dresses and combs her hair.
On the wall there is a scrap of broken glass
Which she uses as a mirror.
If she stands up straight she can see
Her eyes and lips when she puts on rouge and kohl.
If she bends her knees she can see
Her eyes again and her thick, black hair
Which she piles and pins on top of her head.
This is something she does every day.

Rainoo murmurs the English she picked up
In a house in the Persian Gulf.
A yellow-haired Englishwoman taught
The children who listened, sometimes.
Rainoo listened all the time
As she carefully cleaned the schoolroom.
Do you understand, children? Please listen!
Rainoo is listening, aren't you?
Rainoo is good at languages.
This was something the teacher said every day.

There were flowers in the schoolroom.
They used to close when Rainoo touched them.
The master of the house used to touch her.
What didn't he use to touch?
Rainoo used to close like a flower.
She used to close her mouth and turn her head
When he pulled her sari to her waist.
This was something he used to do every day.

Rainoo tucks a rupee inside her bra
For the bus she takes to the brothel.
She walks with a limp from the time
The mistress of the house surprised her
With the master and pushed her downstairs.
This was something she did only once.
Rainoo's passport was stamped with a word for *whore.*
Today Rainoo will speak Marat'hi,

Hindi, English, Arabic and French.
What language won't she speak today?
This is something she does every day.

South District, Prague

One day perfect love could come to me
Like a woman from a crowded bus
Long overdue and driven carelessly
Along an asphalt road wet with rain.

She might travel past untended fields
Which wind has combed so grass lies flat.
I will change the dull, official name
On maps to read *The District of the Heart.*

Today you gesture at the sun sinking
In the windows of the building opposite.
The sky itself seems blank, uncoloured,
The texture of an undyed linen mat.

We watch the glory in the glass spread out
Making concrete seem delicate as coral.
You murmur your favourite English word,
Impossible, impossible,

And refuse my offer of a rose.
How could I explain it to my man?
I wave goodbye at a brilliant smile
On the last bus westwards to a steel town.

One day perfect love could come to me
Like wind blowing snow across the grass.
A shadow with a brilliant smile
Will descend from an empty bus.

Impossible, she'll say as I hold out
Her favourite pink rose and a petal drops,
Then another in the frost. *Impossible*,
She'll breathe, her lips withering my lips.

Incident in Guatemala

Our tour was halted near a river
Whose water the washed-down clay had stained
To the colour of an abattoir.
Trees were snagged on the bridge's stanchions
And it was said that bodies from a killing
Had floated past a week before.

We were lined up and made to stand with arms
Stretched above our heads while our hands rested
On the flaking paintwork of the bus.
A border guard picked through our belongings
And another felt inside a blonde girl's blouse.
A third cocked a rifle, covering us.

We waited while the passport of ourselves
Was opened and stamped upon so we could go
Into a land of outrage beyond our sight
But audible as the girl cried out
And the guards made jokes. Across the border
I asked, uselessly, *Are you all right?*

But she did not answer. Instead she watched
Where light was glossy on plantation acres
Under a narcotic swish of rain
And where it glowed in the sheen of sweat
On arms which raised machete blades
And let them fall on dense, green sugar cane.

At Huwailah Beach

By the village, *Mother of the Pillars*,
We gave a lift to an Egyptian peasant
Whose speech was corrupt with Hindu phrases.
He tickled the back of my neck with a snake

Which he'd hidden in voluminous sleeves.
Not venomous, it sidewound down my shirt.
Its head was small as a fingerjoint
And it coiled on my knees neat as a cat.

The road was dark so we invited him to stay.
Now he rocks from side to side as someone
Picks out *Brown Girl in the Ring* on the oudh
Tapping the striped belly of the instrument.

Fins flicker in the shallows as fish twist
Tugged in by handlines. Soon they will be grilled
And eaten over a quarrel about
Where the best Arabic is spoken

While I go through a box of Kleenex
Since I have the Gulf War all over my feet.

Observing the Sunrise: from a Letter from Russia

1.

I'm on duty today sitting near my father-in-law.
He has cancer, but the operation wasn't radical.

There are only two patients in this ward, the other is between worlds.
He's eaten nothing for days, just drinks, smokes and smells terrible

which is why I'm sitting by the open door to the passage
where I can observe L—'s father. We'll spend the night here.

We must keep an eye on two connections from his body
to a bottle under the bed, a urine collector.

I have a book with me (translated into Russian),
a novel by John Braine called something like The Way Up The Hill.

The British mentality is described rather interestingly,
but having no experience I can't say badly or well.

2.

I had to stop writing. I had something to do or was far too sleepy.
This is the second night I've been here. So my English forgive and forget.

Some patients with tubes from different parts of their bodies
pass me by from time to time on their way to the toilet.

The nurses changed the dressings on that man between Earth and Heaven
(or Hell), He doesn't smell any more. He's almost arrived wherever.

A nurse on call asked me to wake her when he stops breathing.
It's not very pleasant suddenly to have to watch over

a human being's last moments. Yes, he died a moment ago.
I've just told the nurse, Sister Irina, a pretty girl,

and she's gone to ask another to help carry his body away.
Excuse my naturalism. It's a way to escape this world of Peter Breughel.

3.

My father-in-law seems not to have noticed what has happened.
He's one of the most intelligent people in our city.

He was born in Leningrad in 1928.
When the war began he and his sister were evacuated by decree.

But as the result of someone's terrible mistake
they were sent to meet the Germans and their train hit by a bomber.

They escaped safely and got to a village which was not occupied.
He had to work on a kolkhoz and got acquainted with hard labour.

He was going to write a realistic novel about this
and planned to repeat the route they took in 1941.

But he found the documents connected with their adventure
(later evacuations were more successful) had been taken.

4.

Having just bought a car I hoped to take him to his weekend home,
his *Ebony Tower*, where close to nature he hoped to live and write.

He'd built himself a small house there, two by three metres.
He'll hardly use it any more or the boat

in which we rowed to the centre of Lake O – and fished
observing the sunrise. Three or four times a year we must have done this.

I will finish this letter with a small tragedy of my own.
The day before I became assistant to a nurse I tried to purchase

a car radio cassette player from a second-hand shop,
but I found it had been robbed and the radio stolen.

Probably it isn't my karma to have a car radio.
My spelling I have checked. My English forgive and forget again.

A Snail in Istanbul

The sultan of moisture creeps
On a flagstone shadowed by nettles.
He carries his turban on his back
And shows his tentacles, a scholar
Bareheaded out of the mosque.
No doubt his hidden mouth is prim
Though his tongue, rough with hunger
Not prayer, will rasp on greenery:
One foot, one lung, one kidney,
One gonad, mostly male, feminine
Only in summer in a place
The Turkish guidebook labels
The Convent of the Whirling Dervishes.

In the octagon of the dance hall,
On a balcony wall overlooking
The dancing floor is a photograph
Of abandoned holy men, a cluster
Of white frowns with unkempt beards
Like snails stuck to a glossy leaf.
They lingered after Sheikh Galib
The last, great formal poet,
Years after Halit Efendi
Whose body is in a tomb outside.
His head is buried elsewhere.
Their pens and mechanical verses
Are displayed, nibbled by neglect.

On the path the devotee of stealth
Has almost reached the nettles.
His spiral of shell and viscera,
His delicacy, will not be scourged
By the stinging hairs on the stems.
Far above him the curator
Picks tobacco from a lower lip
Before he brushes down the graves
Tilted by subsidence so they seem
Almost imperceptibly to make
A gesture in the dance. Their headstones
Are grey, bearded with inscriptions,
Crested with marble turbans.

In the Country of Birds

A buzzard roosts by the highway
A glum functionary in the parliament of birds
Waiting to raise points of order or prey
Upon a careless puss-in-boots with a gold ring on its tail.

All this happens as storks return unseen
With their human-coloured legs, intelligent eyes
And beaks like the weapons of the scissor men
Who waited in Mother's wardrobe when we went to try her shoes on.

Later there are remote flurries of swallows like poppy seed
Flung against the sky and falling in slow motion,
The nightingale's imitation of everything he's heard,
A collective panic of starlings in the school yard.

Grandmother says it was when cottages stood on magpie legs:
Grandfather dressed a Jewish doctor and his wife
In peasant costume and sent them out with the hogs
To help potato pickers as the Gestapo hunted high and low.

Grandfather hid their jewellery in his house
Until the war was over. One gold ring was lost and a friend.
Perhaps the ring was juggled through a hole by a mouse,
Perhaps a cat ate up the mouse and wore a gold ring on its tail.

A bell ting-tangs from an onion dome
Made of wood and slate. The pungent notes that chime
Summon us to recite our perpetual fall from grace
And a promise of perfection with candle, book and hymn.

I will open a volume of light and shadow
Where two streams meet. When I turn the pages I will go
Up through the forest to where trees thin to rowan and juniper,
Where holy writ is left behind with the jay's bravado.

There in the grass I might find a nest of lark's eggs.
The bird will soar through fear not joy; its song diverts
Come away! Come away! And so I will, just like an ogre,
Rain clouds on my shoulders, striding over hills in seven league boots.

The Fossil

'If necessary we can go back to the desert' –
(Reported of King Faisal during the oil crisis of 1974)

As is the custom we have perched
On thorn bushes a slim haunch
Of mutton and the rice we cannot eat –
Clear of the ground so only birds may feed.

Now under an acacia we sip tea
And watch dust devils skedaddle
Along the highway's grainy liquorice
Between a frail, odd expanse of seedlings.

Here iron giraffes clatter and lean down.
Their unimaginable mouths drink
From levels hundreds of feet beneath
As tankers, their round calves, suck water from them.

Sayer Al Harthy offers me a cigarette.
His robe's linen whispers with the gesture
Like paper tissue drawn from a box.
He has shown me the omega shape

Of stones which form a Bedu mosque
And explained with so few words that I think
Not even enormous wealth can drown
Habits made by economies of thirst.

He points to the fossil I have found,
A bean-sized snail or nautilus
Stone-dry for millennia, and asks
Teacher, tell me, where does this thing come from?

Out of courtesy or cowardice
I answer *From the time of dinosaurs*
And Noah when men prayed to animals
So that God covered the earth with water.

The Drowned Boy

i.m. Munji Mohammed Abu Derbalah

Yesterday wind snarled through the square
As his friends brought chairs and hung out lamps
For mourning in the lee of his flat.
We sat informally in silence
As lights jerked in the gale seeming
To founder in the sand. I bore it
For half an hour while some sat all evening
Preferring respect to comfort.

Today what we are left with is ground
Damped down, pitted with the marks of chairs.
Where the square is dry, pythons of sand
Slide as the wind eddies to stillness.
We taste grit and wait for the sky to clear.
The boy is with habits of saying
Yesterday. He recedes into the words
Of inadequate regret, but remains

An acrid ripeness in our language,
A woodsmoke curling through the village,
A memory whose truth alters
Like perspective among a grove of palms
Where the air is hazy with dust
So the trees seem to form the relic
Of a temple, their branches arching
Broken apses on marble pillars.

How much of him can we take with us?
As much as we take of ourselves.
The future narrows to a catwalk
Over the dangerous places
And reaches boats whose sails are sewn
From winding sheets. They bob on a sea
Calm as brass although now we hear it
Unappeasable, nuzzling the rocks.

Magnolia

In this quiet before the storm I can almost hear the magnolias bloom,
The buds unsheathing in their bracts
To a mass of flamingo heads pointing at a hazy moon

While the street lamp's beam makes the cherry tree's gnarled growing
                                                                    points
Seem webs of branch and twig on which
A raised white stitching means they'll bend soon in lazy, decorous do's
                                                            and don'ts.

Behind the trees lightning tears the night as though it were carbon paper,
Flimsiness ripped by sheer heat,
Blossoms of a million volts over what is right and proper.

You flinch at thunder, at apocalypse, you say God's Will Be Done.
In the morning on the river bank
Police will find a man dead from spring lightning or winter rum.

'It's miles away. We're safe here,' my comfort eddies to glibness
Or patters like the fat drops of rain
As I talk on about the magnolia exhibiting its flawless

Pinks and creams for a week then shedding all to leave armoured fingers,
Green at first and then vermilion
A process of water, nitrogen, hydrocyanins for colours.

We approach the street lamp's beam flawed with the drift and mottle
                                                        of a shower
Our shadows withering into themselves.
I lift my gnarled hands to the light and I watch my fingers flower.

Jane Yeh

JANE YEH was born in New Jersey in 1971 and attended Harvard University and the Iowa Writers' Workshop. She has been awarded a New York Foundation for the Arts Poetry Fellowship and the Grolier Poetry Prize, and was a runner-up in the *TLS*/Blackwells Poetry Competition. She currently lives in England and is at work on her first collection, *Marabou*.

Of the poems included in this collection, 'The only confirmed cast member is Ook the Owl ...', 'Substitution' and 'Vesuvius (in the Priests' Quarters)' were published in *PN Review*; 'Convent at Haarlem' in *Antioch Review* and *PN Review*; 'Shoemaker's Holiday' in *TriQuarterly* and *PN Review*; 'Self-Portrait after Vermeer' in *Grolier Poetry Prize Anthology*, *New Voices* (anthology) and *PN Review*; 'Revenger's Tragedy' in *Poetry* (Chicago), and *Poems, Poets, Poetry* (anthology); 'Correspondence' in *Boston Review* and *Metre*; and 'Telegraphic' in the *Grolier Poetry Prize Anthology*.

The only confirmed cast member is Ook the Owl,
who has been tapped to play the snowy white owl
who delivers mail for Harry

– Article on pre-production for the Harry Potter movie,
New York Post, August 2000

Claw up. Claw down. Cut.
My fine eyes. My fine eyes are – Cut.

I was fluffed and plucked, like a beauty-pageant winner,
Between takes. Like a news presenter.
Could I be a news presenter?

Rider: 5 rashers bacon. 8-oz. tin mixed nuts.
2 lbs. rabbit fillets. Assorted drupes.

Between takes, I did leg-lifts in my trailer.

If asked what is your most treasured possession, I would say
The woolly toy Tracy, my personal trainer, gave me when young.
I learnt to spy it from afar, then swoop down and seize,
But only on cue. Mr Sheep goes everywhere with me now.

If I could wake up having gained one ability,
It would be the capacity for more facial expression.
It is so tedious to have one's beak set in a permanent frown.

My greatest talent is impersonation –
To simulate a person's idea of an owl.
Sadly, I owe my success to typecasting.

My greatest fear is to be found wanting.

At the première party, the women were not very clothed.
It is of advantage to be clad always in feathers.

I allowed fake friends to pet me.
My picture was taken several times with the boy.
I enjoy parties because otherwise I see only Tracy.
Afterwards, you wonder what the glitter was for.

Substitution

First I blindfolded the revolting cat.

I read much lore about chickens: the windowless abbatoir
Found in the French countryside where the slavish Usurper

Had laid her ear to the wall, listening to the sound of innumerable
                                              chickens
Inside; the coop where reject eggs were thrown and hungry chickens

Came running to eat the yolks. When I held her pet chickens
In my sham embrace, they were unable to detect my subterfuge.

I stole objects from her house one by one, replacing them
With lovingly crafted replicas, until she was living in an imitation

House resembling exactly a real one. In the superfluous space
Of my living-room I built a scale model of her haunts

To acquaint myself with her arena of exploitation.
Also I learned to draw small shrews in 1,126 positions.

At her wedding the fishy minister had proposed, enthralled by
Her white-gloved ability to cause fawning. The best man had already

Succumbed to her auras. I did not want
The slavish bouquet thrown by the Usurper, but it was then

That I conceived my elaborate measures.

I elevated my port to an Usurper-esque height.
It was necessary moreover, to expand my

Girth. Before, I had been on a private hunger strike
To protest her fleshy bargains. So even her odd rations I readily
                                              consumed.

I adopted the Usurper's signature scent, Hypnosis.

I deployed her matt brand of lipstick because her kiss is a veiled
Machination. With mock lashes I enhanced my eyes.

Eventually I could not be distinguished from the Usurper. The way to
tell us apart
Is that she is Evil and smiles only at her slaves. Also the way to tell us apart

Is that she is controller of the slaves, which is what I should rightfully be.

Now that the preparations are complete, I do not regret
The rigours entailed by my exquisite method.

I refilled the replacement candy dish with poison

In spherical form. The fabric of the blindfold was spotted black and white,
Like the cat. On it I painted trickily the facsimile eyes.

Convent at Haarlem

> In the seventeenth century, the whitest linen in Europe was
> produced at Haarlem. Strips of fabric were laid out in the fields to
> undergo bleaching and drying.

We go out
Sprinkling bone-ash from long-handled shovels, it is dusk and the seventh

Month of repetitions. Ours is the lengthwise passage
Between March and November; we filter through the dunes

Like rainwater, keeping straight by the linen. In the brownest
Stretch of grass you could come upon me,

Above all scurrying animals and fringed about with water:
Sieved out from a sea off the Low Countries'

Polderlands, slipping the estuaries.
You would judge me a narrow sort of reclamation.

We turn in to our several labours, the spreading of rushes, the winding up
The well. In a house of silent women

You are the rotten timber, the sand that rustles under-
Foot, the crooked tallow candle's socket: yours is the slow

And graduated wearing. Once, I was the one running
Across the green lines of your fields, crossing

The blond-wood boards of the floor of your room, an original
Bit of nonsense, your doll.

Shoemaker's Holiday

> All they that love not Tobacco and Boies are fools.
> — Richard Baines, 1593

Heel-block and stopper, cone of thread, dresser,
The four awls and stirrups, hand and thumb
    Leathers: 'St Hugh's bones' lie spread out before me.
If I am part aether, un-earthly
    Of humour, it could be surmised
My mother was a sempster. Theirs is a guild notorious
    For patience. Yet I am more probable
To yield to temptation. I've a weakness for
    Tea-drinking, for tobacco and boys, for any
Riot of horn-blowers that comes down the street.
    Rubbing-pin, paring knife, bucket
Of nails: if I am, on occasion, a touch
    Temperamental, it might be because I was kitted-out
For frivolity. Flashing of needles and flicker of satin,
    Ribbon-curler, shirrer, an excess of beading –
Notorious angel, I am apprentice to no one.
    I think a little playing up would be forgiven.

Vesuvius (in the Priests' Quarters)

When it came, we were getting ready
For bed. The gowns lay on the mattresses,
White as palms open for a coin.

I always loved how they spread themselves,
Armless and headless, across the sheets,
Loved that perfect stillness of things

Dropped from a great height. They stretched
The length of the beds like so many
Paper dolls. That night

The sandals waited on the floor, soft
Brown mouths, open and dumb as those
Of children. I loved how the feet

Came down with a slap, the straps
An embrace. We were kneeling
When it hit. Through the window

I saw its hand and when the others ran
I stood, walked the row
Putting on each pair of sandals, pulling

One crackling cloth over my head after another.

Self-Portrait after Vermeer

Already I am too old, coming to
An appointment 7,417 days late, penitent

In pearls and homespun, high-waisted, tied up
With muslin: an Old Master. I've got to break

For it and believe
There is another way, that curtains can be drawn

Over windows, voracious
Dreams; somehow

To count slow enough
Under my breath to go

Unseen. I am crouching behind you,
Trying to shrink and failing

Fast. But in this kind of divine
Light I am transfigurable, re-

Formed, chimaerical. There are those who doubt
And those who wait. I will keep coming

Late, playing my age, framing myself
While you steal a little here and now.

Revenger's Tragedy

You don't return my calls. In a month of missing days
Everything thwarts me, even the curls of my hair freeze;

My skin sheds, leaving flakes on my wool sweater. We are erratic
Both, changing with the weather, but you think of it

As an astronomical progression. Last year you called me
Your little sunflower. Eleven blizzards later I think of how

To get you: calculating mercury, sighting along constellations,
Rehearsing the lines of a paid assassin – *not know me, my Lord?*

You cannot choose! I bide time,
Hoarse-tongued and blue as poison, the double

Line of my eyes gone to slits. I hate like a tooth hurts,
At the root. I will startle the bones

From their sockets, they will crack like glass
And catch in your throat. I will dazzle

Your heart from its cage. The lungs will knock and clap
Together in the empty place. The applause will make you rattle.

The Pre-Raphaelites

'What *do* you mean by beauty?' In the Grosvenor Gallery
In our 'medieval' dresses, in our rapt and utterly

Fashionable gazes, we cannot touch
The isinglass wall of these

Damned unprofitable lives. What it is
That wrecks us –
                    I was lying
In the garden, up against the barrier

The mandragora were twined like thin fingers.
Sometimes I pose when no one is there.

Please God I am a creature of habit and well-fed. A puzzle
Like a door in a hedge that is made of hedge, inscrutable.

What it is that is wrong in me –
                    When one glove in a pair is turned inside-out
It becomes the same as the other one, but with the seams exposed.

Nobody wants to see that.
Here is a conjuror's trick:

I the disappearing girl. Look again and I turn up back in the box,
Same as before. I have not got anywhere.

Why am I, why am I caught
In the hinge of this world and it presses me, where was the wrong turn

Taken took me to the middle of the maze and gave
Me this head, these hands, this beast's face?

Correspondence

I've gotten nothing for weeks. You might think of me

As dated in a blue housecoat, buttoning and unbuttoning,
Waiting you out: I have my ways

Of keeping time. When your letter comes, dogs will bark
Up and down the street. The tomatoes in the garden

Will explode like fireworks. Each day the mailman passes
In a reverie, illiterate, another cobweb

Grows across the door. Picture me
Going bald one hair at a time, combing and curling, burning

My hand on the iron once every hour: I like to
Keep myself busy. When I hear from you, *aurora*

Borealis will sweep across the sky. Every lottery ticket in my drawer
Will win. Even the mailman will know the letters

Of your name. If you bothered to notice, you would see me
Turning to gold rather slowly, bone

By bone, the way teeth come
Loose from the gums, the way animals go

Extinct, in geological time.

Telegraphic

The orchids allow for drastic invitation. My last resort

Is cabling you at Spa, where the waters keep their manganese
Secrets below where the fingers of plants taper off

In despair – where you are burrowing behind your silks
And drapery into an elliptical bed, closeted

Among the glass globes' mouths choking with flowers,
Invalid. I have been wasting these two weeks

In an extravagant show of faith, gloved in lavender
And clinging to an ostrich-feather fan, expectant as

The evening primroses in their velvet coats palely
Scattering themselves across the hedge, the bell

On the corner that sounds each hour
When it is not the hour. After you recover

Beneath some canopy of lilies, leftovers
From when the cutting work is through, after

You pick me apart stem by stem
In the porcelain chambers of your head, I will live

On eggshells, chips of bark. You can leave
A new man, not knowing

How I will stick in you: ghost
Limb: wormwood heart.

Love in a Cold Climate

I was the queen. In a game of charades,
Two fingers mean *concealed*. An avalanche
Was in the wings waiting, the beginners
Frozen on their marks waiting for curtain

Up. My internal anatomy is strange
Like an ice floe on the verge of breaking off
That doesn't, a natural disaster
Like two tonnes of mountain coming down on

A trapped cabin. Let's pretend we're alone
In the empty house – one light left, ghostly –
Still holding on, still huddled, for warmth, then

Pretend that I never pretended to you,
Never kept in the dark a second
Body to warm me – *Finis*. Curtain down.

Alchemy

If it could be done, I'd do it
In an instant. I've got the charts,
The mortar and pestle, the fullest
Array of flasks this side of Rome.
My walls are papered with symbols, and the biggest
Is gold. There's a cabinet full
Of rejects: salt and cow hair,
Rye harvested under a full moon and tin,
Magnesium and saints' spit. I could show you
Calculation, the reams of vellum in my closet, enough
Ink for ten octopi. Instead I promise you
Piles of gold, shining heaps higher than
Your bed, weighing more
Than the both of us.

These nights I stay alone, poring
Over books in older tongues; none
Of the words are in my dictionary.
Signs stare down at me – calcium, Saturn,
Silver, lead – mean as Chinese, like a maze.
When I fall asleep I dream the metals
And planets sweep me up, wrap me
In their dark mesh bed and I can't see
To read any more. But I wake to
The jars of cow parts, the cup and balance
Waiting to measure, and the open mouths of flasks
That say *You will still be hungry*
When you are full.